The FX Bootcamp Guide to Strategic and Tactical Forex Trading

Founded in 1807, John Wiley & Sons is the oldest independent publishing company in the United States. With offices in North America, Europe, Australia, and Asia, Wiley is globally committed to developing and marketing print and electronic products and services for our customers' professional and personal knowledge and understanding.

The Wiley Trading series features books by traders who have survived the market's ever changing temperament and have prospered—some by reinventing systems, others by getting back to basics. Whether a novice trader, professional or somewhere in-between, these books will provide the advice and strategies needed to prosper today and well into the future.

For a list of available titles, please visit our web site at www. WileyFinance.com.

The FX Bootcamp Guide to Strategic and Tactical Forex Trading

WAYNE McDONELL

WILEY

John Wiley & Sons, Inc.

Published by John Wiley & Sons, Inc., Hoboken, New Jersey.
Published simultaneously in Canada.

For general information on our other products and services or for technical support, please
contact our Customer Care Department within the United States at (800) 762-2974, outside the
United States at (317) 572-3993 or fax (317) 572-4002.

Wiley also publishes its books in a variety of electronic formats. Some content that appears in
print may not be available in electronic books. For more information about Wiley products,
visit our web site at www.wiley.com.

Library of Congress Cataloging-in-Publication Data:

McDonell, Wayne, 1973–
    The FX bootcamp guide to strategic and tactical Forex trading / Wayne McDonell.
        p. cm. – (Wiley trading series)
    Includes bibliographical references and index.
    ISBN 978-0-470-18770-8 (cloth)
    1. Foreign exchange market.   2. Foreign exchange futures.   3. Speculation.   I. Title.
    HG3851.M43 2008
    332.4'5–dc22

                                                                2008019685

Printed in the United States of America

10 9 8 7 6 5 4 3 2 1

Contents

Preface

"Planning is great matter to a general [forex trader]; it is the ground of death and of life; it is the way of survival and of destruction, and must be examined . . . before doing battle, one calculates and will win, because many calculations were made."
        —A quote from *The Art of War* by Sun Tzu, a
        military general in ancient China. Scholars
        surmise that he lived around 600 B.C.

PLAN YOUR TRADES AND TRADE YOUR PLANS

Why is trading forex similar to war? They are both a zero-sum game. In war, this means kill or be killed. In forex trading, this means that if you make a winning trade, someone else made a losing trade against you or vice versa.

Forex is pure. There is no central exchange in currency trading like there is for equities, such as the New York Stock Exchange. It's simply bulls vs. bears. Hawks vs. doves. Those who think a currency will gain value and those who think a currency will lose value.

Forex has no middlemen, few regulations, and is purely a global community of traders. No one controls the market.

For example, recently the central bank of New Zealand intervened to try to lower the value of the country's currency. It worked for a few hours. Then traders pushed it back up. Traders control this market. No one else.

Why is this good?

Statistics have shown that most traders fail in forex. Some have reported less than a 10 percent success rate for new traders entering the market. However, this is great news for you:

- This means 10 percent of traders make *all* the money.
- Ninety percent of new traders fail because they do not acquire the skills, but more importantly, they lack the patience and discipline to trade successfully.

FX Bootcamp's Guide to Strategic and Tactical Forex Trading will guide you on the path from failure to success. However, the journey is yours to take. The question is do you have the guts to work your butt off and get really good at trading forex?

Not clear enough? How about this?

I believe that 90 percent of amateur traders fail, not because they lack an understanding of the market, but because they are not willing or able to do the work required to become an amazing trader.

In forex trading, patience and discipline are just as important as technical and fundamental analysis.

- Are you willing to give yourself enough time to learn how to trade?
- Are you willing to do the work?
- Will you do whatever it takes to succeed?

This book will help you develop positive trading habits and give you lifelong trading skills. It's not a silly magic system of the moment.

This book will not do the work for you. But it will teach you how to stay out of a lot of bad trades, and you will learn how to wait for the better trades. In fact, this book will to teach you how to think for yourself and trade successfully on your own.

"...this book will to teach you how to think for yourself and trade successfully on your own."

FX Bootcamp's Guide to Strategic and Tactical Forex Trading will help you become a part of the top 10 percent that makes 100 percent of the money. (Blood, sweat, and tears not included.)

WHAT IS *NOT* IN THIS BOOK

Fluff! I assume that you know what a pip is and that forex volume is over $2,000,000,000,000 per day. I'm not going to convince you to trade forex. You should be at or near that conclusion now all on your own.

This book *will* take care of the rest. It will teach you how the market works and how to trade it.

NOTE

For additional educational resources—including training videos, live webinars, chart examples, and more—please visit this book's free companion web site www.fxbootcamp.com/book.

Best regards,
Wayne McDonell
Chief Currency Coach
FX Bootcamp, LLC
www.fxbootcamp.com

The FX Bootcamp Guide to Strategic and Tactical Forex Trading

Introduction

Sun Tzu teaches that there are four stages of planning for victory:

1. Gather intelligence.
2. Formulate strategy.
3. Execute plan.
4. Exit plan.

Creating a trade plan will:

- Help you control your emotions.
- Help you implement your analysis.

By reading the market first and then making logical entry and exit decisions based on your thoughtful analysis *in advance,* you reduce the risk of making a poor trade. You simply set a trap for price. If price falls into your trap, you trade your plan. If it does not, you set another trap and wait. In other words, take the high ground and wait for your adversary to come to you. Do not fight on a level playing field.

Your strategic planning will give you a tactical advantage and you are more likely to be victorious. You are not guaranteed success, but the odds are much more favorable and less risky. By creating a plan in advance and waiting to execute it, you remove a lot of emotion from your trading. You are no longer reacting to the market, you are simply executing your plan. In fact, you will be spending more time waiting for your trade setups than trading. Inevitably, this is less stressful.

Removing emotion will help you avoid stupid trades based on greed and fear. By relying on logical plans, your trading becomes repeatable. By trading when the market is behaving in predictable ways (this is what your plan really is—your prediction of future price action based on past results), you are removing stress.

Stress is a form of risk, and you need to manage it if you are going to succeed on a long-term basis. Imagine trying to trade forex the next 30 years when every time you pull the trigger you start to sweat bullets. Trading like this, you will eventually have an emotional breakdown. Reduce stress!

Planning your trades and trading your plans will reduce a lot of risk—and stress—in your trading career. In addition, conservative, repeatable trade plans will also increase:

- Control
- Consistency
- Confidence

By virtue of the repeatability of your trade planning, you will control your emotions and bring consistency to your trading. Once you are able to trade profitably on a consistent basis, your confidence will skyrocket.

In my experience working with forex traders from more than 50 countries around the globe, I know that confident traders are much more likely to trade their plans.

When traders consistently plan their trades in advance and are confident enough to pull the trigger when they are supposed to, they have a sense of control. It may be an illusion, as the forex markets are chaotic, but think about it this way:

Who do you think the 10 percent of the traders making 100 percent of the money are?

A. The consistent and confident traders with a sense of control because they plan their trading in advance.
B. The traders who pull the trigger based on gut feeling and who react to the market.

WHICH DO YOU DO?

Imagine you are at a cocktail party. People are floating around the room and mingling. We've all been in situations like this.

The group next to you is talking about the latest reality TV show and you've never even heard of it. It sounds so incredibly stupid. What at bore!

I wonder what they would say if you jumped into the conversation with:

"Speaking about being voted off the island, how about those FOMC meeting minutes released this morning? Governor Pool voted to lower interest rates again! We should vote him off the island!"

It's likely that no one would have a clue about what you are talking about. Your life revolves around acronyms such as CPI, PPI, NFP, PCE, GDP and such. They live lives of quiet desperation.

The next time someone approaches you and strikes up a conversation by asking, "So, what do you do?" try using my favorite response.

"I buy and sell money."

Dumbfounded, the individual will respond with, "What?"

"I apply fractal geometry and chaos theory to profit from the global currency markets."

Now the person will be impressed. But don't say, "I'm a currency trader" as people equate this with "gambler" and for the 90 percent of amateur traders who lose money, they'd be correct.

But not you; you are a professional profiteer. After reading this book, you will focus less on trading and more on planning your trades in advance, as you are really seeking opportunities to profit, not to trade.

If the odds are just 50/50, you'll pass as it will be too much of a gamble. You'll wait for a better profit opportunity.

As Sun Tzu would recommend to a military general, I recommend to you, a currency trader:

Take the high ground and wait for your enemy to come to you. You are more likely to have an honorable victory. Even if you take the high ground and lose, because you gave yourself the best odds of winning, you will be able to consider it an honorable defeat. However, if your adversary does not fall into your trap, you simply don't fight and live to fight another day.

In summary, strategic and tactical forex trading is not a system. It's a conservative and repeatable methodology.

Once you have learned, developed, and refined the trade planning skills outlined in this book, you will certainly be on your way to being a part of the 10 percent who make 100 percent of the money. If you are willing to work your butt off, it will just be a matter of time.

Basic Training

The goal for Part One is to develop a common language that you and I can use. The rest of the book will discuss how the technical indicators highlighted in the first two chapters work together to tell a story of what is happening in the foreign exchange (forex) market.

Currency charts use candles and technical indicators to communicate. It is important for you to have a strong understanding of these building block indicators that form the foundation of the trading methodologies discussed in this book.

To learn this language as you read this book, I highly recommend that you take the time to set up your charting package with these indicators and settings so you can practice the methodology. Members of FX Bootcamp have access to a template that makes this easy. Nonmembers will just have to invest a little more time, but it will be worth the effort. Read the book, study the concepts, practice on your demo account, and develop long-term positive trading skills.

In Part One you will learn:

- The difference between a simple moving average (SMA) and an exponential moving average (EMA).
- How to trade moving average crossovers.
- How to use the moving average convergence divergence (MACD) indicator.
- How to trade MACD divergence.
- How to use Bollinger Bands.

- How to trade volatility.
- How to spot a technical reversal.
- How to identify support and resistance (S&R).
- How to trade a break or bounce of S&R.
- How to trade S&R role reversals.
- How to use Fibonacci retracements.
- How to use Fibonacci extensions.
- How to use pivot points.

CHAPTER 1

Lagging Indicators

M ost technical indicators are lagging, which means they are slow. They tell you what just happened ... after the fact. However, by combining historic price action with predictive price patterns, we'll have enough evidence to form the basis of a trade plan.

In this chapter, you will learn how to use technical analysis to read your charts. It is critically important to learn these concepts well. They are key to understanding the market's behavior. The technical indicators we'll discuss do not control the market, but they describe a story of how traders are trading it.

MOVING AVERAGES

A moving average (MA) is an average of a predetermined number of prices (such as closing price) calculated over a number of periods (such as 55 candles). The higher the number of candles in the average, the smoother the line is.

A moving average makes it easier to visualize price action without statistical noise. Instead of watching the up and down behavior of every candle, you are watching the relatively smooth moving average line. Moving averages are a common tool in technical analysis and they are used within all time frames: 1-minute, 5-minute, 15-minute, 30-minute, 60-minute, 120-minute, 240-minute, daily, weekly and monthly candle charts, for example.

It is important to observe that a moving average is a lagging rather than a leading indicator. Its signals occur *after* the new price movements, not before. Moving averages do not think ahead. They tell you what has happened, not what will happen. Nonetheless, moving averages have a critical role to play in properly planning your trades in advance. The past does not always predict the future, but it sure likes to repeat itself.

SMAs vs EMAs

There are two types of commonly used moving averages:

1. **SMA:** The simple moving average or arithmetic mean.

   This moving average is only an average. Add up all the candles that you'd like to measure and then divide by the number of candles you added together. For example, a 21 SMA is calculated by adding the closing price of the last 21 candles and then dividing by 21. Simple, eh?

2. **EMA:** The exponential moving average.

   The exponentially smoothed moving average takes into account more than just the previous price information of the underlying currency. It places more weight on the most recent previous candles. This makes it more sensitive to the most recent price action. For example, a 21 EMA places more weight on the last 5 candles than the first 5 candles.

   The exponential moving average reacts to price changes more quickly than the simple moving average does because it pays more attention to newer candles.

I like moving averages a lot. You will see later in this book that at FX Bootcamp we use several different moving averages at once, but they offer different pieces of the puzzle when planning our trades. When the market is steadily rolling along, moving averages keep us in our trades, but if something changes, such as a moving average crossover, we'll likely get out or trade the new direction.

Moving Average Crossovers

Moving averages are frequently used as price filters. To filter choppy price action into a more reliable indication for true price action, a short-term moving average has to cross a longer-term moving average.

The trade planning methodology we teach in the FX Bootcamp training sessions is to use several moving averages on the chart simultaneously. The most obvious use for multiple moving averages is to watch for crossovers to confirm new trends.

A crossover would consists of a short-term (21 candles) EMA that crosses a longer term EMA (55 candles). Short-term EMAs (fast) are more sensitive to price changes because they are measuring fewer candles. Conversely, longer term EMAs (slow) tend to be more flat and are less likely to whipsaw up and down.

When moving averages do cross, you should take notice. If the fast EMA crosses below the slow EMA, it likely confirms new downward price action. If the fast EMA crosses above the slow EMA, it likely confirms new upward price action. However, such crosses should not prompt you to place a trade, as it often occurs too late and will put you in the market an unfavorable risk/reward ratio. The crossover should have been part of the trade plan that you created in advance, as not every crossover is the same. Moving average crossovers are great because they are easy to see and will attract traders, but they simply do not replace the work of planning your trades.

A simple use of moving averages is using them to gauge the speed and direction of the trend. If prices are held by the 21 EMA, the trend could be considered strong. If prices break the 21 EMA, you should become more cautious. This could be the sign of a reversal or a consolidating market. New rules will apply. We'll discuss this in more detail later in the book, as it is a key concept to trade planning.

MOVING AVERAGE CONVERGENCE DIVERGENCE (MACD)

Moving average convergence divergence, generally known as MACD (pronounced "mack dee") is one of the most reliable and simple indicators in our toolbox. MACD is a trend-following momentum indicator, or oscillator, which shows the relationship between two moving averages of recent prices. An example is shown in Figure 1.1.

The MACD is often made up of three components:

1. **MACD Line:** The actual MACD line is calculated by subtracting a slow moving average (EMA) from a fast EMA. In our example we use the 21 as the fast EMA and the 55 as the slow EMA.
2. **Signal Line:** The signal line represents an EMA, not of price, but of the MACD. In this case we calculate the EMA of our MACD for the last eight bars.
3. **Histogram:** The MACD histogram is the difference between the MACD and its signal line.

MACD just might be the most popular indicator used by forex traders. That is why we recommend that you use it. However, be aware that MACD

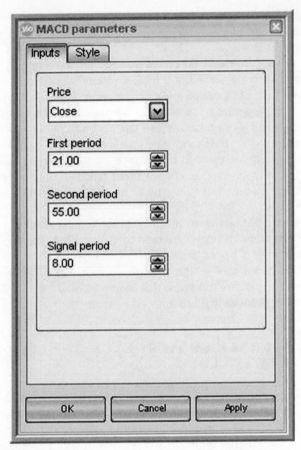

FIGURE 1.1 Moving Average Convergence Divergence (MACD)
Source: DealBook® 360 screen capture printed by permission. © 2008 by Global
Forex Trading, Ada MI USA

is often misused. Like any other technical indicator, you cannot rely on it for trades. It should be part of your entire trading planning process.

How to Use MACD

There are three common scenarios to watch for:

1. **Crossovers:** When the MACD falls below the signal line it is a bearish signal, and indicates that it may be time to sell. Conversely, when the MACD rises above the signal line, the indicator gives a bullish signal, and suggests that it may be time to buy.
2. **Divergence:** When the price diverges from the MACD, it signals the end of the current trend. When the price is rising and MACD is falling (negative divergence), or vice versa, it can be considered an indication of something going on and can be used to predict changes in a trend. That's right, the lagging indicator that is supposed to follow the price is predicting future behavior.
3. **Dramatic Expansion:** When the MACD expands dramatically—that is, the shorter moving average pulls away from the longer term moving average—it is a signal that the currency is overbought/oversold and may soon return to normal levels.

Once again, let me be perfectly clear. All three of these scenarios are important and should not be overlooked. However, none of them are signals to trade. They are opportunities to form trade plans based on likely outcomes commonly generated by such situations.

For example, MACD divergence is tradable only when confirmed by other indicators. It does not always yield profitable trade opportunities. Therefore, if you traded every MACD divergence, just like if you traded every moving average crossover, you would certainly lose money.

However, when planned in advance and confirmed with other technical indicators, success is much more likely. This is because several things are happening at once and each is attracting the same bulls or bears into the trade you are planning.

MACD Divergence

MACD crossovers and dramatic rises are easy to spot. However, spotting MACD divergence takes a little practice. Figure1.2 shows some examples of charts that display MACD divergence signals.

What does this divergence mean? Just that the current price trend is running out of steam. In this case, you'd create trade plans based on

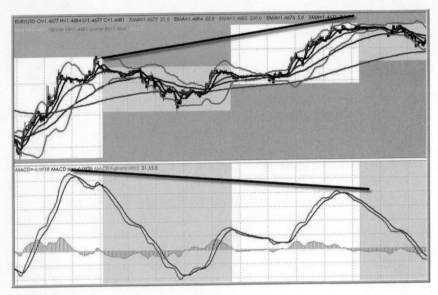

FIGURE 1.2 Examles of MACD Divergence
Source: DealBook® 360 screen capture printed by permission. © 2008 by Global
Forex Trading, Ada MI USA

reversal patterns, moving average crossovers, or other indications to consider a trade in the opposite direction. It may not happen right away, but
MACD divergence can be a powerful hint that the market is changing.

What you are looking for is when price action and MACD do not agree.
For example, if price is making a series of higher highs and MACD is making a series of lower highs, something between the two is out of sync.

I see MACD divergence as a sign that fewer and fewer traders are in the
trend. No one is trading against the trend—yet, but fewer and fewer traders
are in the trend. I'd guess that traders are getting nervous and slowly fading
out of their trades.

When the only traders in a trade are nervous, they are likely to exit
their trade at the first sign of trouble. So if MACD is diverging from a
bullish trend, as soon as the bears muster up enough guts to short, the
bulls will exit and the bears will take control. This is exactly why MACD
divergence can be so powerful. When it works, it often works well, but it
takes time to set up.

There are two powerful keys in locating possible times where divergence is likely to represent a reversal in price.

1. **Support and Resistance:** MACD divergence can be powerful when
   price is at double tops or double bottoms. Just as you are creating a

trade plan based on a bounce or break of S&R, you spot MACD divergence, which is a sign that current price action is running out of steam. This would indicate that there are not enough committed traders to break S&R, so perhaps you should focus your trade plan on a rejection reversal. See Figure 1.3.

2. **Exhaustion Pullback:** The second is when an oscillator, an overbought/oversold indicator, has reached its overbought/oversold range and is turning back down to normal. You may often see the MACD lines extremely overbought or oversold. This is *not* a reason to trade. In fact, it indicates signs of strength.

Remember this: "Of course it's overbought; everyone is buying!" Don't confuse the overbought or oversold MACD zones as trade opportunities. However, when *price* reaches its extreme, where it's gone too far too fast, you will see price exhaust and the MACD lines drop back into the normal zone. This is often a better signal. See Figure 1.4.

Combining an exhaustion MACD pullback with MACD divergence at a double top, you would have a second cross of the MACD and an opportunity to trade.

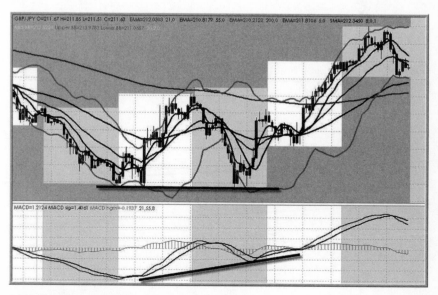

FIGURE 1.3 MACD Divergence Trending Up
Source: DealBook® 360 screen capture printed by permission. © 2008 by Global Forex Trading, Ada MI USA

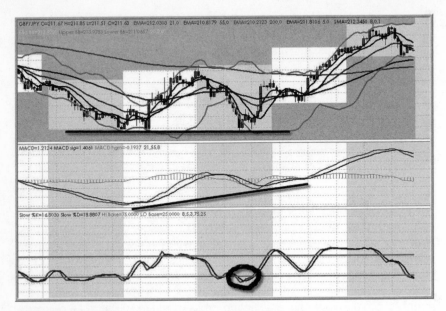

FIGURE 1.4 MACD Divergence with Stochastic Trigger
Source: DealBook® 360 screen capture printed by permission. © 2008 by Global
Forex Trading, Ada MI USA

Those two situations, along with your other tools can provide excellent
trading opportunities. It is also important to note that divergence can be
found not only on the MACD line and signal line as was demonstrated in
the previous examples, but it can also be found on the histogram, as shown
in Figure 1.5.

BOLLINGER BANDS

As forex traders, we rely on market volatility as a means to profit. We want
to see changes in a currency pair's price. When the market produces a
consistent, repeatable move up or down, we want to earn pips from that
change in price level.

Volatility is the relative rate at which the price of a currency pair moves
up and down. In other words, it's the amount of price change over a period
of time. If price moves up and down rapidly over short time periods, the
market has high volatility. If the price changes very little, the market is
exhibiting low volatility.

As you've probably noticed, if you've stared at your charts long enough,
the forex market tends to find itself in one of two basic conditions: range

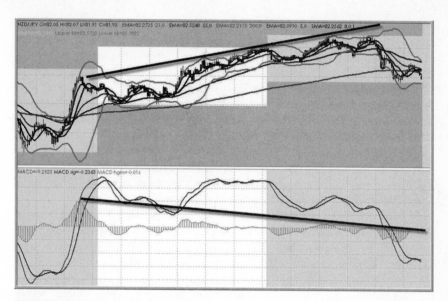

FIGURE 1.5 Divergence in a MACD Histogram
Source: DealBook® 360 screen capture printed by permission. © 2008 by Global
Forex Trading, Ada MI USA

bound or trending. By some estimates, the market is actually range bound
about 70 to 80 percent of the time. In this scenario, the bulls and bears are
in a battle that neither side is really winning or losing.

Price action is back and forth, back and forth—much like a tennis
match. While in a range, the market establishes a fairly consistent level
of volatility. When price is trapped in this range-bound condition, we'd
like to have an idea of where it is likely to reverse from up to down (or
vice versa).

Eventually, volatility kicks in and the market deviates from its range-
bound state.

Think DEVIATION = TREND.

Price is deviating from the current norm—trending beyond its recent established range. When such a break occurs, we'd like to have some sort of
early-warning indication that the move above or below the recent range is
a significant deviation from the norm.

Volatility Indicator

The Bollinger Bands (BB) indicator was first introduced in the 1980s
by John Bollinger, a longtime technician of the market. These bands,

calculated based on standard statistical theory, estimate the probable high and low price of a currency pair, given the market's recent level of volatility. The bands are drawn at equal distances above and below a simple moving average.

Think of Bollinger Bands as an envelope indicator, projecting top and bottom lines around price. The bands act like mini support and resistance levels. The longer the time frame you are in, the stronger these bands are.

These bands are self-adjusting. When the market becomes more volatile, the Bollinger Bands expand or open up and move in opposite directions from each other. Whenever price enters a tight trading pattern, the bands respond by contracting or moving closer together. In a range-bound market, the bands are usually parallel to each another.

To better understand the story told by Bollinger Bands, consider a seismometer used to measure the seismic waves generated by movements in plates under the earth's surface. The seismograph's pen makes waves on a paper chart. The waves drawn vary in size relative to the size of the earth's "quake."

When the earth's surface is calm, the seismograph draws small waves within a tight range, and the width of this range is relatively small—much like the narrow and parallel Bollinger Bands during a range-bound market.

When an earthquake strikes, the ground shakes, and wide curves of varying size are drawn on the chart reminiscent of the widening Bollinger Bands one sees during a fast-trending market.

How to Use Bollinger Bands

There are three different ways you can set up trades with Bollinger Bands:

1. **Range Trading:** When these envelope lines, or bands, are parallel to each other, they can be used to predict levels at which to enter or exit a trade. The Bollinger Bands have identified a range within which you can consider trading.

   As a general rule, when price reaches the upper band, the market is considered to be overbought. When price touches the lower band it is considered to be oversold. However, a touch of the upper Bollinger Band is not in and of itself a sell signal, and a touch of the lower Bollinger Band is not in and of itself a buy signal. Remember, you're seeking opportunities to profit not opportunities to trade!

   In other words, do not predict a support or resistance level based solely on a Bollinger Band. Instead, wait for price to bounce first, and seek confirmation from other indicators before entering a trade. You may create a reversal trade plan at extreme Bollinger levels, but like any trade plan, you'll need confirmation before execution of the plan.

After entering a trade following a reversal, your can place your stop on the other side of the Bollinger Band.

2. **Breakout Trading:** When prices break above or below the upper or lower band, it is an indication that a breakout and trend is about to develop. To filter out false breaks, we recommend seeking confirmation of the move using a momentum indicator, such as a 5 EMA/8 SMA cross or a stochastic cross.

    If the move is a break above resistance and to the upside, you're seeking to enter a long trade while price walks up the upper Bollinger Band. If the move is a break below support and to the downside, you'd like to enter a short trade while price walks down the lower band. In either case (going long or short), your exit would be determined a limit order or a moving average cross.

3. **Tunnel Trading:** When you see that Bollinger Bands have become tight and narrow, watch for a breakout to occur in the near future. The longer and more narrow the tight Bollinger Bands, the greater the breakout will likely be. It's predictive, so pay attention. Also, this is only true when the market is moving, such as 5 A.M. to 5 P.M. London time. Tunnels during the odd hours of forex simply show you that no one is trading at all, and a breakout is not likely to happen until they return to their charts.

    Some traders refer to this scenario as a "Bollinger Band Squeeze." When the breakout occurs, a new trend, or deviation, is started and the Bollinger Bands begin to spread further apart. This is an excellent clue to plan a trade around. If the plan is successful, you have a nice Bollinger Band breakout trade, and you'll be walking the bands into profit.

Bollinger Band Settings

Figure 1.6 shows the settings for the Bollinger Bands we display on the charts displayed during the live coaching sessions at FX Bootcamp.

The default setup on your trading platform for Bollinger Bands is likely 20 periods and 2 standard deviations and one we've found to work effectively on forex charts.

Omission of the Middle Bollinger Band

Why do we remove the Middle Bollinger Band from the charts we display during FX Bootcamp sessions?

We like to keep things as simple as possible in Bootcamp, and that goes for the number of lines on our charts as well. Each Currency Coach

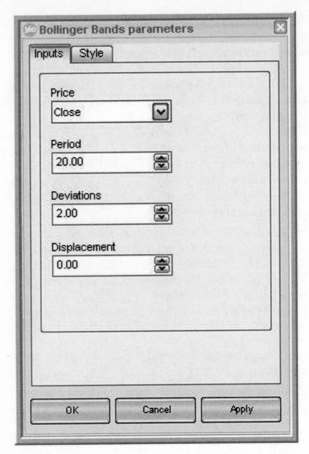

FIGURE 1.6 Bollinger Bands
Source: DealBook® 360 screen capture printed by permission. © 2008 by Global Forex Trading, Ada MI USA

already uses several other moving averages, so we've chosen to omit the middle band. The middle BB is actually the 20 SMA, similar to the 21 EMA already shown on our standard chart template.

Calculating the Bands

This is the simple formula for this volatility indicator:

$$\text{Upper BB} = 20 \text{ SMA} + 2 \times (\text{standard deviation})$$

$$\text{Lower BB} = 20 \text{ SMA} - 2 \times (\text{standard deviation})$$

STANDARD DEVIATION

Standard deviation is a measure of the spread of a set of numbers. More specifically, it measures how widely data values (in the case of forex charts we are measuring recent closing prices) are dispersed from the average of those values.

The larger the difference between the closing price and the average price, the higher the standard deviation and volatility of the currency pair. The closer the closing prices are to the average price, the lower the standard deviation or volatility of the currency pair.

According to statistical theory, when the market is in a range-bound condition, roughly 95 percent of recent closing prices are contained within two standard deviations of the moving average.

Think about this concept in simple real-world terms. Consider a market that is range bound and price pops above the upper Bollinger Band. Price does not belong there; it is out of its element. Under these ranging conditions, price will fall back within the standard deviation 95 percent of the time. Not an ideal time to go long.

SUMMARY

The indicators in this chapter are visual representations of various mathematical studies of price and time. MACD is nothing like stochastics. Bollinger Bands don't have much in common with EMAs. However, they all have one thing in common: They are all lagging indicators. They study what happened in the past. Therefore, they are slow and do not tell you what is happening right now, and they certainly do not tell you what will happen in the future.

Wouldn't it be nice to have a crystal ball indicator that could predict the future? It's every trader's dream. Well, here's your dream come true! In Chapter 2, I will review three leading indicators that help predict the future: support/resistance, Fibonacci retracements/extensions, and pivot points.

Leading Indicators

As mentioned in the first chapter, most technical indicators are lagging, which means they are slow. They tell you what happened after the fact. However, we also have three leading indicators that help you predict future behavior.

Sure, there is no magic crystal ball that can help you see the future. But the tools outlined in this chapter can help you set realistic future profit targets based on prior price action such as pullbacks into a fast moving trend or yesterday's trading range.

PRICE SUPPORT AND RESISTANCE

Support and resistance (S&R) are terms used by technical traders to refer to currency pair price levels at (or near) which price has reversed its direction in the past, or where price is likely to reverse due to psychological reasons.

In our FX Bootcamp sessions, we may suggest at times that a rising currency pair will likely find resistance in a certain price zone. This is a predicted near-term high for price—a ceiling—where buying pressure will likely encounter a larger degree of selling resistance. If such a resistance zone holds, then there are many sellers at that particular price, and they may overpower the buyers (who may turn into sellers themselves). Price will dip as long as this selling pressure is present.

Likewise, we also suggest at certain times that a falling currency pair will likely find support in a certain price zone. A support area represents a

21

"floor" of sorts where traders expect the buyers to support or hold off the market's selling pressure. It is a predicted near-term low, and price will rise as long as this buying pressure is present.

Why Is Price S&R Important?

Support and resistance levels are a very powerful part of your forex trading arsenal, applicable to both trending and range-bound markets.

In a range-bound market, support and resistance define the lower and upper bounds of price movement. In such a market, we may consider trading opportunities of selling at resistance and buying at support.

When price approaches resistance, we may begin to look for signs that price will be rejected at that level and reverse back down. When it goes down toward support we expect to see price bounce back up off of that support level. This process of bouncing off of support and being rejected by resistance will continue until the range is broken.

In a trending market, we look to support and resistance as levels where we would enter a trade if price can successfully break through S&R.

In both cases, if we have valid reasons to trade, either a bounce/ rejection or a break of the support and resistance lines, such price action at S&R provides us with a great opportunity to take a trade with reduced risk.

Why is that? The answer is that once price successfully breaks a support or resistance line, they often switch roles and what was once support is now resistance, and what was once resistance now becomes support.

Identifying Price S&R

Support and resistance is actually found on charts in many different forms. Price channels, fib levels, trend lines, psychological levels, horizontal S&R lines, and even moving averages all represent support and resistance to one degree or another. Some are more specialized versions of support and resistance, and their strengths vary depending on current market conditions.

To mark price S&R on your charts, a horizontal resistance line is established by connecting at least two significant high prices occurring at approximately the same level. A horizontal support line is drawn by connecting two or more significant low prices occurring at approximately the same level.

General S&R Rules

1. **The more it holds, the tougher to break**: The more often price tests a level of resistance or support without breaking it, the stronger the area will be.

2. **Role Reversal**: When price breaks above a resistance level, it is common to see that level change its role and become a new area of short-term support.

For example, in Figure 2.1, the dotted line represents a level of resistance that has prevented price from moving higher on two prior occasions (points 1 and 2). Once the resistance level is finally broken, however, it becomes a level of support (as shown by points 3 and 4).

Similarly, when price breaks below a support level, support often "becomes resistance." In Figure 2.2, the dotted line indicates a support level which has kept price from moving lower on two previous instances (points 1 and 2). However, once the support level is broken, it becomes a resistance level (as illustrated by points 3 and 4).

1. **Long-term trumps short-term**: Support and resistance levels on longer term charts (for example. 1-hour, 4-hour, or daily charts) tend to be stronger than those determined by inspection of a 15-minute chart.
2. **Don't overdo it**: There are two things to be careful of when working with support and resistance. The first would be identifying too many support and resistance lines. Having too many S&R lines can prevent you from entering the market when the market is ranging or lead you

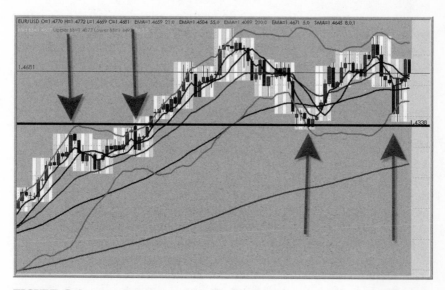

FIGURE 2.1 Upward Roll Reversal
Source: DealBook® 360 screen capture printed by permission. © 2008 by Global Forex Trading, Ada MI USA

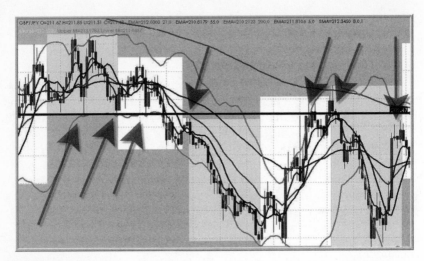

FIGURE 2.2 Downward Roll Reversal
Source: DealBook® 360 screen capture printed by permission. © 2008 by Global
Forex Trading, Ada MI USA

to believe that a breakout has happened before it actually has. Try to identify major areas of support and resistance and work with those instead of trying to identify every area where price paused.

The second item to be careful of would be working with obscure S&R lines. As with much of technical analysis, S&R levels work because traders use them. When identifying areas of support and resistance, focus on those that are obvious.

FIBONACCI RETRACEMENTS

The Fibonacci sequence has a mathematical ratio that appears over and over in nature as well as in art and engineering. Having met so many traders from around the world, I am always surprised by how many of them don't use "Fibs." In fact, many traders have told me that don't believe Fibonacci theory, that it is just a bunch of hocus pocus.

To a certain degree, they are correct. The vast majority of the traders I have met who shared their negative opinion about the use of Fibonacci theory had traded other markets, such as equities, for many years. Their experience has told them that Fibs don't work. They certainly may be correct. They traded in markets much different from forex.

For one thing, forex is many times larger than any other financial market. In fact, it is many times larger than all the other financial markets combined. Perhaps these equity traders didn't find Fibonacci theory helpful in their trading because the market they traded was just too small. I also think that the stock market is much less efficient, so it doesn't surprise me they don't use Fibs. I am surprised, however, by how many traders think their experience in one market will lead to success in another market, even though the two markets may be quite different. They are not open to making the required adjustments and may find forex frustrating.

Fibonacci ratios are one tool to apply when trying to understand very large sets of data that are so complex that they seem chaotic. Chaos theory works well in forex because the currency market is so massive and so efficient.

There are so many variables that can affect the forex market because it is a global, liquid, and efficient market. Almost everything matters in forex (geopolitics, weather, news) and will have an instant impact, big or small, on the value of currencies. How can someone even begin to understand something that is always changing because everything changes it? This complexity makes forex the perfect medium for chaos theory and Fibonacci ratios.

So people began to study the complexity of forex, presumably to profit from understanding its behavior, and applied some of the mathematics they used in studying complexity in the natural world, such as spawning and population growth of salmon. Its likely that big banks hired math whizzes, such as quantitative analysts, to make sense of the endless variables affecting forex valuations. As more "quants" studied forex complexity and chaos theory tools, Fibonacci ratios stood out as useful.

Now I can't tell you if they worked extremely well when Fibs were first applied to forex, but I can certainly tell you they work now. Do Fibs work because the forex market is complex enough to apply this kind of Chaos Theory, unlike other markets such as equities? Most likely. Do they work in forex because so many traders use Fibonacci ratios when they trade? Absolutely yes!

In trading, application of the Fibonacci ratios have been found to be useful in helping to determine possible market turning points. Forex Traders use Fibonacci Retracements to try to predict Fibonacci Extensions. The ratio of the pullback will help predict the outcome of the extension. In simple terms, the theory uses past price behavior to predict future price behavior, based exclusively on ratios developed by Leonardo Fibonacci back in 1200 AD

What Are Retracements?

To understand what Fibonacci retracements are, we need to review what a price retracement is.

A trending market is defined as price moving in one direction or another, either up or down. Price does not make these moves in a straight line. An uptrend, for example, is a series of higher highs and higher lows. Price usually returns to old price levels before moving on in the direction it is going. This returning to previous levels is known as retracement.

Fibonacci retracements are a method of using specific Fibonacci ratios to define how far back price may return before moving again in the direction of the trend.

We use the following four ratios in our daily training sessions:

0.382

0.500

0.618

0.786

How Are They Used?

Now that we have some idea of what Fibonacci retracements are and what ratios we'll be using, we need to know how we actually use them.

In the case of an uptrend we watch as price makes new highs. When we see that price is stalling at a given price or hitting an area of suspected resistance, we would want to measure the distance from the current high to a previous swing low.

The price distance between those two points is then separated into the 38.2 percent, 50 percent, 61.8 percent and 78.6 percent values, and lines are drawn on the charts at those levels. On most charting platforms this is done simply using a Fibonacci retracement tool.

Measured this way, a 61.8 percent retracement is when price falls 61.8 percent between the previous swing high and low before resuming its uptrend. It comes a long way back but is heading back up again, presumably to make another higher high. Conversely, a 38.2 percent retracement in a downtrend can be seen when price rises about a third of the distance between the recent swing low and swing high before it continues its way down the charts.

Think about it as walking up a steep hill of sand. You take three steps forward and then you slide two steps back. You do this over and over again, slowly climbing the dune. In general terms, your sinking steps are making 61.8 percent Fibonacci retracements. It's a slow pace, but you will eventually make it to the top. You are making progress and you are trending upward. See Figure 2.3.

Technical Reversal

There comes a time when a retracement is no longer a retracement. It's just returned too far to hope that it will continue back in the direction of the prevailing trend. There is a line in the sand that says, "If you cross

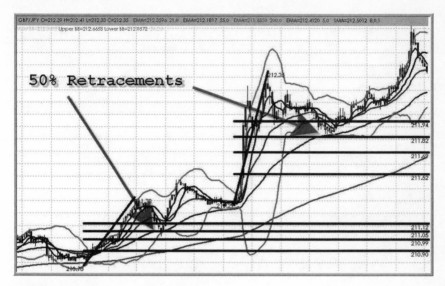

FIGURE 2.3 Fibonacci Retracements
Source: DealBook® 360 screen capture printed by permission. © 2008 by Global Forex Trading, Ada MI USA

this area, you are no longer a retracement but a reversal." That line is 78.6 percent.

The reason for this is that the pullbacks that return this far into the prevailing trend are just too stressful for the traders to try to ride out the trend. They suffer through the pullbacks. The greater the pullbacks, the more the traders are likely to wimp out.

Just imagine you placed a trade and you were up 45 pips in profit. Everything that put you into the trade plan still looks strong, so you decide to ride out the first pullback and see if you can get into a trend you can ride all day. After some time, as price is pulling back, you see your profit dwindle down to only 10 pips. Are you still confident? My guess is that your charts will not look so certain anymore. Do you cash out while you still have some profit? If traders take the money and run, the trend will bust and reverse.

Therefore, if price crosses the 78.6 percent line, technically speaking, it's a reversal. For an example, see Figure 2.4.

Risk/Reward

One man's trash is another man's treasure. The flip side to a 78.6 percent retracement is that if the trend is very strong, such a large pullback could be a great place for traders who are not already in the trade to jump in.

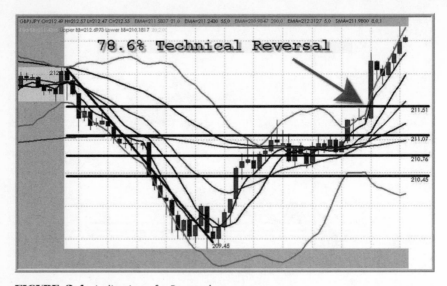

FIGURE 2.4 Indication of a Reversal
Source: DealBook® 360 screen capture printed by permission. © 2008 by Global Forex Trading, Ada MI USA

Since the 78.6 percent Fibonacci retracement is the line in the sand for a reversal, if price shows signs of holding at this level, it's the cheapest place to enter the trade and catch the prevailing trend.

The best thing about this kind of entry is that if you are wrong, you can't be very wrong. If price does not resume in the direction of the trend and breaks the 78.6 percent line, then you've lost very little, as you entered near the 78.6 percent line.

By entering a trade at the 78.6 percent Fib level, you are hoping that other traders also see this retracement level as an affordable entry, either attracting new traders to the trend or having traders add to their winning positions. Either way you are buying cheap and risking little.

If the retracement attracts bargain hunters because the trend is so strong, then the trend will continue. It's not the perfect trade, but it may be the best risk/reward ratio you'll see when you've already missed the boat.

Fibonacci Fatigue

The one thing to note here is that the farther price retraces, the more it is slowing down. Imagine a strong trend. Everyone is jumping in and trading with the trend. In trading frenzies like this, you don't see much of a pullback in price. You see breakout, trend, pause, breakout, trend, pause, breakout and so on. Traders are so excited that they see the pauses as places to jump in.

FIBONACCI EXTENSIONS

Fibonacci extensions are the opposite of Fibonacci retracements. While traders look to Fibonacci retracements to find turning points in price that are good, low risk areas to enter the market, they look to Fib extensions as a means to project possible exit points *in the future*. These extension levels are usually produced with the same tools one uses to draw Fibonacci retracements.

Fibonacci Profit Targets

Fibonacci extensions are used in conjunction with Fibonacci retracements. They balance each other like yin and yang.

A Fibonacci extension study predicts one thing: how far the trend may continue. It's a leading indicator. It attempts to predict the future based on ratios. Using the previous example of walking up a hill of sand, if you have been taking three steps forward and two steps backward, Fibonacci would predict that your pace would remain constant. Your next progression up this hill will be three steps up and two steps back. Well, I know that doesn't seem amazing, but wait until how you see it work on your charts!

You simply measure the previous swing high and swing low. You are assuming price will continue in the direction of the prevailing trend. If you are in a series of higher lows and higher highs, then you are expecting price to extend higher. If you are in a series of lower highs and lower lows, then you are expecting price to extend lower.

How far will price extend beyond the swing? That depends on how far it retraces. Table 2.1 is a cheat sheet.

TABLE 2.1 Fibonacci Extension Targets by Retracement Level

Fibonacci Retracement	Fibonacci Extension Target
38.2%	161.8% and beyond
50.0%	138.2% to 161.8%
61.8%	121.4% to 138.2%
78.6%	100.0% to 121.4%

Source: FX Bootcamp, LLC (www.fxbootcamp.com)

Here are some examples of how you can use the above table in your trading:

- If you observe a 78.6 percent retracement before price continues in the direction of the trend, Fib theory predicts that the 100 percent or 121.4 percent would be possible profit targets.
- If you see a retracement to the 38.2 percent Fib level, you might want to choose the 161.8 percent extension level—or possibly beyond—as your profit target.

Of course, extension levels tend to be even more powerful when they overlap with other support or resistance indicators. The presence of such overlaps can help you further justify the profit targets you select using Fib theory. Therefore, if I see a Fib level and pivot level overlap, I'd be extremely open to taking profit there. See Figure 2.5.

Pivot Point Analysis

Pivot points were developed by pit traders, who work directly on the floor of the exchange, out of the simple necessity of needing to stay calm during the chaos of "open outcry" trading.

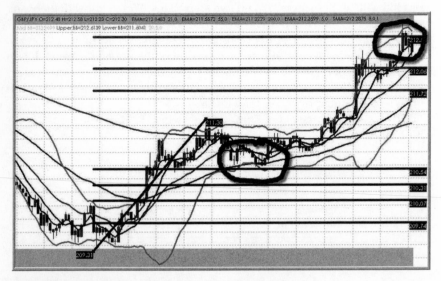

FIGURE 2.5 Fibonacci Level and Pivot Level Overlap
Source: DealBook® 360 screen capture printed by permission. © 2008 by Global Forex Trading, Ada MI USA

According to the Public Broadcasting Service (PBS) web site, "The Chicago Mercantile Exchange packs in more than 4,000 traders and staff on two trading floors each day. In the daily activity of open outcry auctions, minute-by-minute deals are made in heart-pumping theatrical display: a blur of hand signals and shouts, bodies vying for attention and making deals for billions of dollars at lightning speed" (www.pbs.org/itvs/openoutcry/trading.html).

Without a logical system in place, in the chaos of trading in exchange floor pits, emotion would eventually creep into the actions of the traders. The methodology that promoted order and became the norm for these traders was pivot point calculations.

A Brand New Day

In the calm before the storm, a pit trader would review the previous trading day's statistics, such as the price at which the market opened and closed, as well as the previous day's high and low price. With this data, and some basic calculations, the trader would derive likely levels of support and resistance in *today's market*. The trader would write these S&R levels on the back of the day's order cards.

The instant the bell rings and trading beings, the chaos and emotions return to the pits. However, as prices and orders are being shouted back and forth in the pit, a trader quickly scans the back of his order cards before entering a trade. It keeps logic within hands reach.

A Leading Indicator

This quick and simple method was successful in preventing buy orders at the top of the market and sell orders at the bottom of the market. Over time, as more and more traders began using these simple calculations in their trading, the support and resistance levels became pivotal. Not only would price respect these levels, they often reversed because so many traders were entering and exiting their trades at these levels.

The predicted support and resistance levels became pivots points in the market because of the behavior of the traders. Pivot points are a self-fulfilling prophecy. They only work because traders use them not because of fundamental supply and demand. However, because the calculations are done at the beginning of the trading day, yet predict the top and bottom of the market for that day, they are a leading indicator.

Pivot points give you a good idea of the top and bottom of the day's trading range—at the start of the day! They are your radar screen. They help traders spot their target for either entries or exits.

Market Support and Resistance

Pivots are support and resistance for the market. Instead of buying at the top and selling at the bottom, traders began buying at the bottom and selling at the top. They were able to control their emotions by creating trade plans based on their order cards for the day and waiting for logical trading points for those orders.

In essence, pit traders were not reacting to the chaos on the trading floor of the exchange. They brought logic to their trading by planning their trading day in advance.

Pivot points may seem very similar to support and resistance, but they are quite different. S&R is a subjective study of prior price action. Pivot points, in contrast, are not subjective at all. They are a mathematical study of yesterday's market.

Support & Resistance: Price Study: Subjective

Pivot Points: Market Study: Mathematic

Calculation of Pivot Points

The primary pivot number, and the basis for calculation of all other pivot numbers, is the central pivot point. This is very simply the average of the high, low, and close of the previous day.

$$PP = (HIGH + LOW + CLOSE)/3$$

Once the pivot point for the day is calculated, another formula is used to calculate the resistance pivots (R1, R2, and R3) and the support pivots (S1, S2, and S3). "Range" is the difference between high and low.

$$S1 = (2 \times PP) - HIGH$$
$$S2 = PP - RANGE$$
$$S3 = S2 - RANGE$$
$$R1 = (2 \times PP) - LOW$$
$$R2 = PP + RANGE$$
$$R3 = R2 + RANGE$$

Make sure to always use the same 24 hours in your calculation, such as 12 A.M. EST or 12 A.M. GMT, and so forth. At FX Bootcamp, we use 8:00 A.M. Tokyo time. Another extremely popular time is 5:00 P.M. New York time, because that is when banks and brokers close their books.

Note that pivot points are weighted to the close of the market. If yesterday closed lower than it opened, the central pivot point will adjust lower, too. The central pivot point is not just the middle of the previous daily range, it also tells you the direction, similar to a compass.

S&R Pivots

All of the support and resistance levels are calculated off the central pivot point. These pivots are often exhaustion or reversal areas, but they can also provide breakout opportunities just like support and resistance lines created from price action.

M-lines

The M-lines are midpoints between the support and resistance pivots. These are midpoints between pivots:

M4 is in the middle of R2 and R1.

M3 is in the middle of PP and R1.

M2 is in the middle of PP and S1.

M1 is in the middle of S2 and S1.

SUMMARY

They may not foretell the future like a magic crystal ball, but leading indicators sure can be a helpful guide. They can help you foresee likely tops and bottoms well before you reach those levels.

Later in this book, I will show you how you can use these leading indicators to either enter a trade or exit a trade by creating a trade plan with these levels in mind. Do these future levels, potential tops and bottoms, always work as predicted? No. That is why we use lagging indicators as well. Together, lagging and leading indicators paint a more complete picture.

In any case, both lagging and leading indicators are simply mathematical studies of price action. This is called "Technical Analysis." They explain what has happened and perhaps where price is likely to go as a result. However, they do not explain *why* price is behaving the way it is.

Fundamental Analysis is the study of economic data. This information is what moves the currency market: It shapes trader bias. It is what makes people bearish on the British pound, bullish on the Japanese yen or such. Bias, or the net sum of the opinion of all traders, is why currency values change.

It would be a strategic advantage to understand how traders will likely respond as the market changes over time. Smart traders understand that they do not impact the market as individuals, therefore they do not trade as individuals. They study the market to identify "herd mentality" and join the crowd. This strategic analysis is the subject of Part Two.

PART ONE SUMMARY

Following are the key takeaways for Part One:

- Support and resistance identify the boundaries in ranging markets.
- A break of support or resistance can identify continuation of trends.
- Support can also become resistance and vice versa, reversing roles on breaks.
- Drawing too many support and resistance lines can easily become confusing.
- MACD is an indicator made up of three subindicators, only one of which is actually the MACD. The other two are signal line and histogram.
- MACD is traded primarily off of line crossovers, divergence, and when we see extreme differences between signal line and MACD (also shown as dramatic increase in histogram bar length).
- Divergence can be a powerful tool but needs confirmation as it is a leading indicator and can at times lead price action by quite a bit.
- Bollinger bands are a useful tool. However, they should not be used in isolation, but in combination with other indicators to justify your trading decisions.
- Bollinger Bands indicate the current level of volatility in the market.
- Markets move from periods of low volatility to high volatility, or from range bound to trending and back.
- The longer and more narrow a Bollinger Band tunnel, the bigger the breakout.
- Bollinger Bands can be used as both a reversal and a breakout indicator but must be used with other analysis tools to filter out the false breakouts and false reversals.
- Fibonacci retracements are derived from a naturally occurring number sequence.
- Fibonacci retracements can be used to project likely turning points in a market when the market is moving opposite the overall trend.

- While Fibonacci retracements are used primarily for trade entries, Fibonacci extensions serve mainly as trade exit points.
- Use Fibonacci studies to identify possible profit targets. Make use of other significant sources of support or resistance to help define stronger possible exit points.
- Pivot points help locate tops and bottoms of a market in advance.
- Successful traders use both lagging and leading indicators together.

Strategic Analysis

I n the following chapters, you will learn how to create a bias for a currency pair based on solid data. Bias helps you stay on the long-term trend because you see the big picture. It's not a study of candles, but the study of global money flow, economic performance, and central banking operations.

In Part Two, you will learn:

- How to conduct fundamental analysis.
- How inflation affects interest rates.
- How global money flow affects forex.
- How to read Producer Price Index (PPI), Consumer Price Index (CPI), Non-Farm Payrolls (NFP), and other reports.
- How the Federal Reserve Bank operates.
- How central bankers drive currency values.
- Why China and Japan want cheap money.
- How interest rates create carry trades.
- How currencies correlate with each other.
- How currencies correlate with commodities.
- Why to trade the global reserve currency.

CHAPTER 3

How to Gather Market Intelligence to Formulate a Trading Strategy

T his chapter is about strategy. It will not help you get into or out of a trade. However, it will help you logically plan your trades by helping you to focus on gathering intelligence to formulate a course of action.

SPY PLANE VIEW

Strategy is not employed in the trenches. It is not hand-to-hand combat. It is not the foot soldier peering through his sight. It is not the field officer scanning the terrain with his binoculars. It is the four star general reviewing images from the U2 reconnaissance planes and spy satellites . . . away from the battlefield.

In forex, strategy does not put you into a trade. However, it is your general bias for a currency or currency pair. It helps you pick direction for the market. Strategy can last a very long time: many months and often even years. Like a battle commander who uses information to coordinate a cohesive strategy for his troops, a forex trader must use information to formulate a strategy for making trades.

To formulate a strategy in war, analysis of the enemy's strengths and weaknesses—such as its ability to resupply its forces and defend its fortifications—is necessary. The best way to do this is to get constant data from the field. Snapshots from high altitude give telling signs, but they are only clues.

You may see, for example, a convoy of trucks, but you will not know what they are carrying inside them. Is it weapons of mass destruction, troop reinforcements, medical supplies, or civilian refugees?

As a forex trader, you can review all known information to formulate a strategy. You can also get snapshots from a distance in the form of economic data released on an ongoing basis from all the major economies around the world. These data reports are clues to economic strength or weakness.

However, they are only clues—pieces of a puzzle. They are not black and white. They measure a specific economic element, collected in a specific manner, and calculated in a specific method for a specific period in time. They are subjected to huge variations and revisions. They can also be old news. We are often more concerned with the future economy. Do you really care about last quarter's gross domestic product (GDP) numbers and how well the economy was doing three months ago, or are you more concerned with what may happen in the next three months? Nonetheless, they are clues and over time begin to add up.

For example, in 2007, September retail sales in the United States were very disappointing. Many analysts were expecting big sales numbers resulting from back to school sales. However, the weather was quite warm that month and all the sweaters the stores had stockpiled for the cooler autumn months simply didn't sell. The data reflected poorly on the health of the economy. By looking just at this retail data, some experts thought consumers were afraid to spend their money ... or perhaps they were broke. This interpretation could encourage some traders to short the U.S. dollar because the poor retail sales report was a sign of weakness in our economy.

However, if there had been a cold snap and early winter the following month, the sweaters might have flown off the retailers' shelves and we would have seen huge retail sales figures in the ensuing months. This would suggest to economists and traders that perhaps things were not so bad after all and strength would return to the U.S. dollar.

Can you see how simply reacting to "good numbers" or "bad numbers" can have you placing trades all over the place—long one day and short the next? How often would you be going the wrong way?

You need to step back. You cannot see the entire battlefield from your foxhole. You need to see the forest for the trees. Take the high ground and plan your trades around the big picture.

INFLATION SENSATION

All economic announcements boil down to one thing: inflation. It is the enemy of central banks around the world. They combat inflation with interest rates. Interest rates are like a big money magnet. Inflation, and in turn interest rates, are what drives global money flow.

Inflation → Interest Rates → Currency Demand = Higher Valuation

Inflation is never a good thing. It makes prices rise. It can make prices rise in one of two ways:

1. **Everyone is rich.** Inflation of this sort occurs when everyone is doing well. They are happy and confidently spending their money. Times are good.

   Because so many people are doing well and buying things, demand for goods and services is high. When shortages occur, prices rise ... sometimes out of control.

   For example, in 2003 when interest rates in the United States were just 1 percent, money was cheap. A loan from a bank was very affordable. Therefore, vast numbers of people started to buy homes ... sometimes several of them. Hey, why not? Money was cheap and easy to get.

   Demand for existing homes skyrocketed. Demand for new homes skyrocketed. Prices for both followed suit. This inflation of home prices was created by the fact that so many people had a lot of money.

   Currently, the opposite is true in the U.S. housing market. Money is harder to get and is no longer cheap. Demand for purchasing homes is now low. Prices will fall. In November of 2007, housing prices had dropped more than 4 percent year over year. That is the largest annual drop in prices since the 1980s!

2. **Money is worthless.** Inflation of this sort is similar to the previous example of good times, as prices also rise, but not because people are doing well.

   It occurs when people lose confidence in the currency. When this happens, the value of the currency falls.

   If one dollar only buys half of the goods and services it used to, have the prices doubled or has the value of the currenccy fallen by 50 percent? Does it really matter? Either way, you have to spend more to get less because people are not confident in the currency you are spending. If a shop owner feels he could not use the money you are offering him today to make an equivalent purchase tomorrow, you'd have to give him a lot more money today to make it worth his while.

   I've read stories about post-WWI Germany when the Deutsche Mark was almost worthless and inflation rampant. People needed a wheelbarrow full of money just to buy a loaf of bread. Can you imagine that?

CENTRAL BANKING

As you can see, rampant inflation is never a good thing. Central banks (the national bank in charge of the economy for each individual country) combat inflation by adding or subtracting money from the economy. They can do this in many ways, but the most visible method is by controlling interest rates.

INFLATION TARGETING

Some inflation is good, but it should be controlled, not allowed to run rampant and out of control. Central bankers want people to feel confident in the economy, their jobs, and their money. They don't want "the irrational exuberance" that Alan Greenspan, then chairman of the U.S. Federal Reserve, famously attributed to the early days of the dot-com era, but simple confidence in the future.

Current Federal Reserve Chairman Ben Bernanke, President of the European Central Bank Jean-Cleade Trichet, and Masaaki Shirakawa, governor of the Bank of Japan, do not publicly subscribe to "inflation targeting." However, they do outline a comfort level for inflation for their economic policies.

I see this as inflation targeting, but they don't admit to it. In any case, a target or comfort zone gives the market participants a better understanding of how the central bankers will manage the economy. Bernanke is a big fan of inflation targeting, and he is fighting to make it an official policy. I believe that he'll be successful and that the other bankers will follow suit in time.

The markets do not like surprises. The markets like certainty. The more transparent the banks, the more stable the economy ... or so the inflation-targeting philosophy goes.

For example, if the Federal Reserve Bank of the United States is targeting an annual inflation rate of 2 percent but the economic data shows an actual growth rate of prices at 3.8 percent, the Fed will need to do something to slow the growth and rising prices before inflation spirals out of control.

COST OF MONEY

Are prices high because there is too much money in the economy? Too many people are too rich and spending too quickly? Something must be done.

In a real-world example, if you were the manager of a local car dealership and you couldn't keep the cars on the lot because you were selling them faster than you could resupply them, times are obviously good. But how can you make money and pay your employees if there are no cars to sell?

What would you do to manage the situation? You would likely raise prices on the cars and slow demand a bit. You would attempt to align supply with demand. If demand is too high, you'll have an empty car lot. That won't make your salespeople happy. If you raise prices too much, you'll slow demand too much as few people could afford your vehicles and your supply of cars will rise.

You want a balanced strategy. You want to make a small change and see if it makes an improvement. Better, but not quite? Make another small change and see how that helps. Remember, you are seeking balance and steady growth, not a shock to the system.

So what would you do if you were in charge of the U.S. economy and it was also red hot like the car dealership? Raise prices, too? Likely!

You would actually increase the price of money by raising interest rates. This makes money more expensive because it will cost more to borrow from a bank, to get a mortgage, and to charge on a credit card. Consumers would likely slow down their spending. It will also spur businesses to take on less debt and slow their spending, too. They don't like the high cost of borrowing the money, either.

Decreased spending from consumers and businesses will dampen demand for goods and services, bringing supply/demand closer to balance. Retail sales, orders for durable goods, ISM (data reported from the Institute of Supply Managers) and eventually GDP will show the reduction in spending.

But just like the car dealer, you don't want to raise the price of money too much or too quickly. You don't want people to stop spending. You just want the economy to grow in a controlled fashion—perhaps 2 to 3 percent per year for a developed economy. If consumers and businesses stop spending, the economy would collapse, businesses would collapse, the stock market would collapse, and we'd be stuck in a depression. Depressions are not easy for anyone to fix. Slow and steady growth is the goal of central bankers.

MONEY MAGNETS

Interest rates are giant money magnets. They attract money from all across the globe. This can help the value of a currency to appreciate.

For example, let's say you moved to a new town and need to choose a new bank to deposit your money in. There are only two banks in town. Both are on the corner of Main Street and 1st Avenue, directly across from each other.

They also happen to be equidistant from your home, have helpful staff, and offer comparable services. They are both great banks and differ only in one aspect: interest rates.

- Main Bank offers 3.5 percent interest on your deposits.
- 1st Bank offers 4.25 percent interest on your deposits.

All else being equal, most people would choose the bank that pays them the most money for depositing their savings into the bank. This is especially true for large companies, hedge funds, and even countries, each with billions of dollars of cash on hand. Is the interest rate differential of 0.75 percent (4.25% – 3.5%) a big deal? If you are talking about billions of dollars, yes! It's a huge deal. Well, if you consider millions of dollar of extra profit a big deal, that is.

On an international scale, things are basically the same. Central banks pay money for deposits. Some economies want to attract money and raise their interest rates to compete for your investment, much like a local bank may.

Other central banks would like to discourage investment into their economies and could lower interest rates. Lower return on investment is less desirable if you could easily get higher yields elsewhere.

INTERESTED IN VALUATION

Why would a central bank want to discourage investment into its economy? What could possibly be the advantage of that? Lower valuation of its currency! How? It's all supply and demand at work again. First, let's explore the cause and effects of supply and demand.

Remember the car dealership that is selling cars faster than the factory can make them? The high demand actually raises prices. The same is basically true with money.

Let's take the New Zealand dollar as an example. It has a high interest rate. As I'm writing this book, the Bank of New Zealand is paying an interest rate of 8.25 percent!

Simply placing money in the Bank of New Zealand yields a nice profit, considering it's not an incredibly risky trade. You would not likely loose much sleep because you are worried there will be a civil uprising, *coupe d'état*, or other civil, political, or financial unrest.

Generally speaking, New Zealand is a stable country with a stable economy. It's based on British Common Law, has freedom of the press, and democratically elects is government. It's not a crazy place to put your money. Yet it pays a high interest rate.

At this time, you'd be lucky to get close to 2.25 percent from a bank deposit in the United States, so 8.25 percent would be a great return on your cash. This is exactly why big investors like hedge funds love New Zealand.

FOREIGN EXCHANGE

Imagine all the investors and traders around the world moving their money to New Zealand to grab the 8.25 percent interest rate. The purchasing power of this global group is amazing: perhaps hundreds of billions of dollars worth of investment capital spread across all the currencies of the world. However, they cannot place their dollars, pounds, yen, francs, euros or such into the Bank of New Zealand. They can only deposit New Zealand dollars into their accounts.

Before investors from all around the globe place their money into the Bank of New Zealand, they must exchange their local currency for New Zealand dollars. This means they must to buy New Zealand dollars.

DEMANDING CONSEQUENCES

Now let's return to the car dealership example. If the dealer is selling cars faster than he can get them, then demand for the cars is high and this pushes up the prices. When demand is high, prices rise (as shown in Figure 3.1).

When demand is high for a currency, the value of the currency rises. In this case, the investors from Sydney, Tokyo, Moscow, Dubai, Zurich, Berlin, Paris, London, New York, Rio de Janeiro, Chicago, San Francisco and every major city in between all have to buy NZD to get the 8.25 percent interest rates. When they are all doing this, the demand for NZD is high, and this drives up the value of the NZD. See Figure 3.2.

This is exactly what happened in 2006 and the first half of 2007. Interest rates were high, investment flowed to the island nation, and the value of the New Zealand dollar skyrocketed.

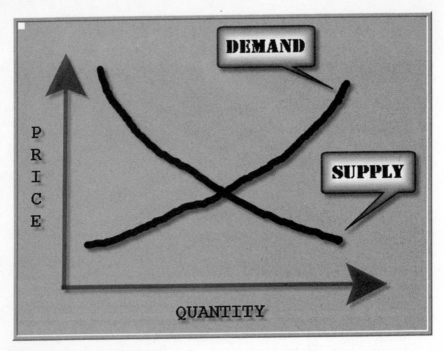

FIGURE 3.1 Supply and Demand
Source: FX Bootcamp, LLC (www.fxbootcamp.com)

HOUSE OF CARDS

However, if all the investors begin cashing out their investments and return their money to their local currency, the NZD would fall, because they are essentially selling NZD to buy their local currencies. For an example, see Figure 3.3.

This is an example of how fragile the carry trade can be. The NZD lost almost all the value it gained in one entire year in just one month. The NZD has fallen in value, not because the New Zealand economy is in trouble, but because investors are removing their deposits . . . mostly to cover losses in other financial investments, such as the U.S. subprime debacle.

NOT INTERESTED

But why do some central banks offer low interest? It is because they do *not* want demand for their currency. Remember, the higher the demand for a currency, the higher its valuation. This is not always wanted.

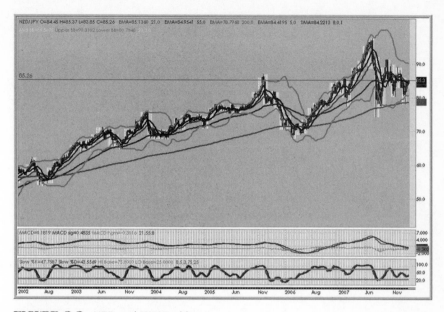

FIGURE 3.2 NZD and JPY Weekly
Source: DealBook® 360 screen capture printed by permission. © 2008 by Global Forex Trading, Ada MI USA

If a currency has a high valuation, it will cost more for foreigners to purchase the currency. Let's say you are a business and sell a lot of products to foreigners via your web site. If your local currency valuation is high, then by association, your products cost more for your customers to purchase, because they must convert to your currency, which is expensive for them to do.

Case in Point: China

You may have read a lot about China. The United States is pointing its finger at China and accusing it of manipulating its currency to make it artificially low. Why would China want to do this? It is an exporting nation. Its economy is based on selling products to foreigners.

If its currency is cheap, then it is affordable for foreigners to purchase Chinese goods and services. If China allows the value of its currency to rise, it will cost foreigners more money to purchase Chinese money, thereby making Chinese products and services more expensive for its customers. The products may be the same price in the local currency, the yuan, but it will just cost more to buy yuan.

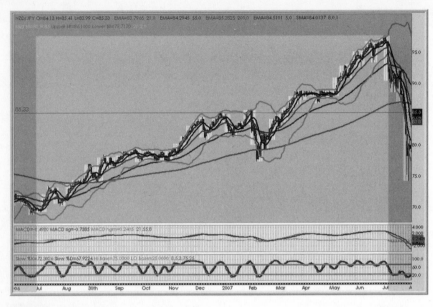

FIGURE 3.3 NZD and JPY Daily Crash
Source: DealBookFigure® 360 screen capture printed by permission. © 2008 by
Global Forex Trading, Ada MI USA

Case in Point: United Kingdom

This is a very real example for any Americans visiting England.

Consider a family who leaves the farm for a trip to New York City. They may be stunned at what a drink at a bar or in a hotel room costs. A small apartment likely costs more than their farmhouse. This is simply because of the high cost of city living. Lots of people live in a very small area, so demand for everything is high.

As with any big city, London also has a high cost of living. However, now take into account currency valuation for foreigners visiting this great city. If the family from the farm visits London instead of New York, they will be in for a big surprise. Not only is this big city expensive, but the Great British Pound (GBP) costs two U.S. dollars (USD) to purchase. Therefore, all things being equal, London costs twice as much as New York City for an American family to visit.

However, the reverse is true. British families can visit the States and everything seems half price to them. Perhaps we'll see a lot of Brits at Disneyland?. The point is that the high cost of the GBP will deter Americans from visiting the U.K., but the low cost of U.S. dollars will attract foreigners to visit the U.S. or buy American products and services.

Case in Point: Japan

Japan is the second largest economy in the world. Like China, it is an exporting nation. This means that Japan exports more—way more—than it imports; largely electronics and automobiles. Japan, because it sells so many products to economies outside of its borders, prefers to keep its currency (JPY) cheap.

Sony, for example, doesn't want its laptops to cost more than Korean or Chinese laptops, simply because the Japanese yen is expensive. Sony directly benefits from a cheap Japanese currency.

How does Japan make the yen affordable? If you buy NZD you will earn 8.25 percent interest. If you by JPY you will earn 0.5 percent interest ... yes, just a half of a percent.

Which one is more attractive for investment? Clearly the New Zealand dollar offers much greater return on investment. This means that demand to buy the Japanese yen has been very low for the last couple of years (with the exception of late 2007 when the JPY dramatically increased in value. Its rise had nothing to do with Japan, its economy, its interest rate, or such fundamentals. This was caused by the sub-prime crash in the United States, an anomaly, not "business as usual." In the next chapter I discuss why the JPY gained so much value so quickly, despite the lack of justification from Japan's economy.). This historically low demand, even negative demand, dropped the value of the currency.

Is it a bad thing? That is a difficult question to answer, but in the scope of our topic, I'll say at least the Japanese exporters are happy, and Japan is an exporting nation. There are many more exporters than importers. It'll just cost the Japanese more yen to buy non-Japanese goods.

SUMMARY

So as you can see, global interest rates set by central banking policy have a major impact in the currency markets. High interest rates attract investment and increase the demand for the local currency and drive up its value. Interest rates are very slow to change, so they often create long-lasting trends.

We've also learned in Chapter 3 that some economies, specifically those that export a lot of goods and services to foreign economies, actually want their local currency to be as cheap as possible. This stimulates their exports and is good for their economies.

Currency trading, boiled down to its essence, is trading appreciating currencies vs. depreciating currencies. As we've just discussed, these value changes are often orchestrated by central banking policy. As they slowly adjust interest rates, they create long-term trends. So, when creating a trade plan, it's often good to look at the interest rates of the currencies you are trading.

Trading a currency from an economy that is in a trend of raising interest rates vs. a currency from an economy that is in a trend of lowering interest rates is at the heart of what we do: strong vs. weak. However, did you know that you actually earn the interest as a forex trader? Many new traders do not know this. If you buy the NZD/JPY, you will earn the interest that New Zealand will pay you for your deposit, minus interest you must pay the Japanese for the money you borrowed from them.

New traders are so focused on pips, they do not even consider the interest earned by currency trading. Hedge funds, in contrast, often don't focus on the pips and will carry their positions as long as possible to earn the interest. This is called the "carry trade," and we will examine it next in Chapter 4.

The Carry Trade

C entral banking and interest rate policies are incredibly important to all forex traders. Interest rates directly affect global money flow, and money naturally finds its way to the highest interest rate economies. How can you trade like a hedge fund manager?

Borrow cheap money to trade with!

Take out a loan from the Bank of Japan. It only charges you a half of a percent (0.5 percent). That's a cheap loan, eh? Now use that money to trade with. You'll still have to pay the loan back plus interest, but it's essentially free money. See Figure 4.1.

What do hedge fund managers do? Let's say the manager has a billion USD of client money. The manager can borrow $25,000,000,000 USD or more worth of Japanese yen from the Bank of Japan depending on leverage (example assumes just 25:1).

This loan costs the hedge fund 0.05 percent in interest payments. Now the manager converts the yen to NZD and puts it into the Bank of New Zealand. As discussed, the investment earns 8.25 percent annually. The interest rate differential, the difference between the interest earned and interest paid is 7.75 percent.

Bank of New Zealand pays the fund:	8.25%
Fund pays the Bank of Japan:	0.50%
The fund profits:	7.75%

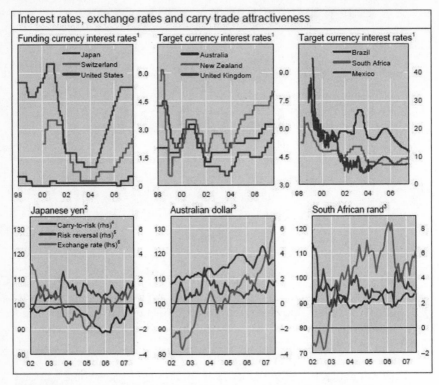

FIGURE 4.1 Interest Rates, Exchange Rates, and Carry Trade Attractiveness
Source: Bank for International Settlements (www.bis.org)

That is great ROI! This trade, based on the interest rate differential is called a "carry trade." Investors, such as hedge fund managers, stay in the carry trade as long as possible—perhaps years. They get paid the interest if the market goes up or down. It doesn't matter. They are guaranteed to receive their interest payments seven days a week no matter what!

Essentially, what you are doing is converting yen to New Zealand dollars. This has a profound effect on the global economy in general and the currency markets specifically. When you convert your JPY to NZD, you are selling your Japanese yen to buy New Zealand dollars. Remember, this was an extremely popular investment vehicle with the big money investors, so there were a lot of traders buying NZD and selling JPY.

What happens when there is huge demand for a currency? The value of the currency rises. Therefore, the NZD would rise.

What happens when there are lots of people selling JPY? Just like anything else, when supply is high, its value falls. This is exactly what an exporting nation wants: a cheap currency to make its products seem more affordable to its overseas customers. In the first half of 2007, the JPY was extremely cheap.

Or in reverse; if a Japanese car costs $35,000 in Canada, that price isn't likely to change day by day like currency valuations do. Let's say the Canadian dollar (CAD) gained 10 percent value in the last few months against the Japanese yen. The car still costs the same, so it makes little or no difference to the buyer. However, when the car maker returns the Canadian dollar back to Japan, it receives 10 percent more yen than it used to.

This looks good, as the manufacturer can say profits from car sales in Canada have risen by 10 percent. Sounds great, right? Sure, but in reality, the company sold just as many cars as it used to and at the same price in Canadian dollars. However, this foreign money was converted into more JPY than before. Hey, more money is still good, eh? Well, it may seem to be, but it buys less and less.

So, generally speaking, when interest rates are high, investors are attracted to put their money into that economy. To do so, they must convert their investment into the local currency of that country. When they do so, this drives up the demand and therefore increases the valuation of the currency, much like eager buyers can drive up the price of a hot stock.

If a central bank doesn't want a high valuation for its currency, it can simply lower interest rates and reduce demand for its currency. In the case of Japan, which actually had zero percent interest, this actually created negative demand.

Investors, like hedge fund managers were borrowing JPY in massive quantities, and they were then exchanging (selling) it for other higher yielding currencies or assets. All this supply of JPY dropped the valuation of the yen even further. Everyone was selling JPY.

FREE HOUSE

How would you like to live your home for free? Let me use an example of a carry trade to illustrate the point.

You own your own home and have a mortgage with an interest rate of 5.5 percent. Your loan is $500,000 You convince the Bank of Japan to lend you the same amount of money. They charge you 0.5 percent for the loan and ask for $5,000 USD as collateral (100:1 leverage is the standard for retail forex traders). You now have $500,000 USD worth of Japanese yen. You then convert the Japanese yen into Australian dollars (AUD) and deposit the money into a bank in Australia.

Australian banks pay you 7.25 percent interest. Not too bad. However, you must pay for your loan for the yen.

The Bank of Australia pays you:	7.25% interest.
You pay the Bank of Japan:	0.50% interest
You profit:	6.75% interest

You then use the profit from the interest rate differential to pay the interest on your home's mortgage.

You earned 6.75 percent from your AUD/JPY carry trade. Your home's mortgage costs you 5.5 percent. You still profit 1.25 percent!

So now your home's mortgage is free. Not too bad, eh? However, an interest-free loan doesn't make your home free, does it?

There is more to a carry trade than just interest payments, but it is what fuels the fire. Why? It is because you are earning interest on the leveraged money.

In the above example, you are profiting 6.75 percent (AUD interest minus JPY interest) on the $500,000 in currency you borrowed, not the $5,000 you used as collateral. This would give you a profit of almost $34,000 if you held the trade for a year. That is a 675 percent annual return on investment. Is your 401(k) doing that? Never in a million years! This is why hedge fund managers *love* the carry trade.

Guess what? It gets even better. We haven't even discussed the potential profit from the appreciation of the AUD. All we discussed was the difference in interest rates earned and paid.

Let's return to the idea that a lot of big money uses carry trades. This created huge demand for the high-yield currencies, such as the NZD, AUD, and GBP (nicknamed the Kiwi, Aussie, and Cable) during 2006 and early 2007. Virtually all of the carry trades are funded with the Japanese yen, as it is by far the cheapest to borrow.

All the buying of high-yield assets drives up valuations. All the selling of the low-yield assets drives down the valuations. You have both forces working for you.

What does that mean to you? Not only do you get to keep the difference in interest rates from the AUD/JPY, but you also keep the pips as well! The pips are worth even more than the interest, so believe it or not, the positive interest rate differential is only the icing on the cake.

SCARY CARRY

Hedge fund managers will try to get their stop losses to break even and they will leave them there for as long as possible. Remember, they want the interest. As long as the price is above their stop loss, they will get paid interest every day regardless of what the market does. This is why a carry trader wants to stay in the trade as long as possible. You can set it and walk away.

Because carry traders are long-term investors, it is very common to get your trades up many hundreds of pips . . . if you're lucky, even thousands. However, as reassuring as this may first appear, at some point you'll get more scared about the pips and forget about the interest.

You'll tell yourself, "Who cares about the interest? If I cash out now, I'll have earned more money in pips that I could make in many months of collecting interest payments. Why not get out now?" This is extremely common at certain psychological levels, such as 250.00 was for GBP/JPY.

This is how carry trades become vulnerable. It's common for a snowball effect to take place. Some traders are worried about a psychological level and react emotionally by taking profit. This reverses the equation and the JPY gains some strength.

Then the technical traders see the pullback at the psychological level and some of them take some profit . . . more JPY strength is created.

All of a sudden, the floor drops and the carry trades collapse all at once like a house of cards. More traders cut out, then more, then even more. Suddenly everyone is jumping ship on these long-term investments.

For example, on July 22, 2007, the GBP/JPY was worth as much as 249.99. At the end of the week, its low point was 239.72. This is a difference of 1,000 pips!

The next two weeks were steady. In fact, the week of August 12, 2007, had a high price of 239.72 but a low price of 219.29. Yes, that's right . . . more than a 2,000 pip drop in one week. In fact, half of that was in just one day. It's true! On August 18, 2007, the GBP/JPY fell more than 1,000 pips. Insane!

This shows that the carry trade creates a herd mentality. You can spook the traders and they can all panic. Why does the JPY gain strength in this situation? It's simple. Let's return to the AUD/JPY example.

POWER YEN

The carry trades start to fall, so you cash out. This means you remove your money from the Bank of Australia. Before you can bring your money home, you must repay your loan back to the Bank of Japan.

Since your loan is in yen, you need to exchange your Australian dollars for Japanese yen to repay your loan. You are now selling AUD and buying JPY. Selling AUD lowers the value of the Australian currency. Buying JPY raises the value of the Japanese currency.

As a consequence, if you live in the United States and make a profit on the pips from your AUD/JPY carry trade, you will also convert the extra yen into USD. This repatriation of profits back to the American economy can also raise the value of the greenback.

This is a great example of global money flow based on interest rates.

$$USD \rightarrow JPY \rightarrow AUD$$
$$USD \leftarrow JPY \leftarrow AUD$$

So as you can see, interest rates are extremely important to currency traders. It's what drives global money flow and creates long-term trends in the forex markets.

SUMMARY

Isn't it interesting how important interest rates are to our forex trading? It really is fundamental to what we do. Luckily, you can study the same data as the central bankers who set interest rate policy. You can read the same reports, crunch the same data, and develop a trading strategy based on how you think central bankers will manage interest rates in their economies. This is called fundamental analysis and is the subject of Chapter 5.

Forex and the Fed

B ecause central bankers control interest rates, we are greatly interested in their actions regarding raising, lowering, or keeping interest
rates the same. Remember, they conduct their interest rate policies
based on inflation and must constantly study economic data for signs of
inflation. Luckily, we have access to this information, too.

With it, we can analyze the same data and ponder, "What would the
head of the central bank do if he saw this data?" We can then develop our
own long-term bias for that currency. The study of economic data is called
fundamental analysis.

Chapter 5 will focus on fundamental analysis and central banking
policy.

FOREX ECONOMICS

The most popular inflation reports for the U.S. economy appear on a regular monthly basis. These reports include:

- PPI: Producer Price Index.
- CPI: Consumer Price Index.
- ISM: Institute Supply Management index.
- Retail sales.
- Housing.
- Durable goods orders.
- NFP: Nonfarm payrolls.
- GDP: Gross Domestic Product.

Any one announcement is usually not that important in the long run. However, it's the trend that is important and how many of the different announcements agree.

For example, if we see inflation rising in most of the monthly reports over a series of several months, we may develop a bias for that currency as we assume the central bank is considering an interest rate hike to combat the inflation. Higher interest rates will attract more investors, create demand for the currency, and the valuation of the currency will likely rise.

Producer Price Index—PPI

The Producer Price Index is a collection of indices that measure price changes from the producer's perspective and how the producer's cost of materials may be passed over to the consumer. PPI covers three areas of the production process: industry-based, commodity-based, and stage-of-processing-based companies.

PPI is a good indication of potential increase in inflation. If producers are having to pay higher prices for their materials, then there is more likelihood that some of those increased costs will be passed on to the consumer, which in turn can affect CPI.

Recent PPI response per currency pair is shown in Figure 5.1. PPI average market response for EUR/USD is shown in Figure 5.2.

Consumer Price Index—CPI

A measure released by the Bureau of Labor Statistics (www.bls.gov/cpi) examines the weighted average of the prices in a basket of goods and services. The calculation of the CPI measure is accomplished by taking

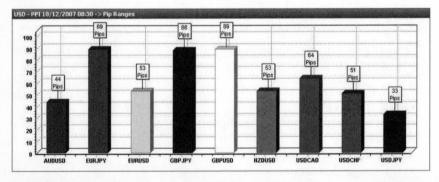

FIGURE 5.1 PPI Response per Currency Pair
Source: NewsTrader Pro | Wincorp Consulting Company | www.newstraderpro.com

(USD) PPI Price Summary 8:30 AM to 11:30 AM							
View by Symbol ▼	Select All Release Records ▼						
Date	Act	Con	Diff	Revised	High	Low	Range ˄
⊟ Symbol: EURUSD							
10/12/2007	1.1%	0.5%	0.6%		32	-21	53
9/18/2007	-1.4%	-0.3%	-1.1%		24	-7	31
8/14/2007	0.6%	0.1%	0.5%		2	-20	22
7/17/2007	-0.2%	0.1%	-0.3%		15	-7	22
6/14/2007	0.9%	0.6%	0.3%		24	-19	43
5/11/2007	0.7%	0.6%	0.1%		33	-17	50
4/13/2007	1.0%	0.7%	0.3%		14	-52	66
3/15/2007	1.3%	0.5%	0.8%		23	-10	33
2/16/2007	-0.6%	-0.6%	0%		17	-24	41
1/17/2007	0.9%	0.5%	0.4%		38	-13	51
12/19/2006	2.0%	0.5%	1.5%		37	-13	50
11/14/2006	-1.6%	-0.5%	-1.1%		27	-52	79
10/17/2006	-1.3%	-0.7%	-0.6%		30	-15	45
9/19/2006	0.1%	0.3%	-0.2%		54	0	54
8/15/2006	0.1%	0.4%	-0.3%		81	0	81
7/18/2006	0.5%	0.3%	0.2%		25	-57	82
6/13/2006	0.2%	0.4%	-0.2%		46	-18	64
5/16/2006	0.9%	0.8%	0.1%		44	-10	54
4/18/2006	0.5%	0.4%	0.1%		47	0	47
3/21/2006	-1.4%	-0.2%	-1.2%		12	-69	81
2/17/2006	0.30%	0.20%	0.1%		74	-7	81
1/13/2006	0.90%	0.40%	0.5%		47	-10	57
12/20/2005	-0.70%	-0.50%	-0.2%		1	-88	89
11/15/2005	0.70%	0.00%	0.7%		37	-14	51
10/18/2005	1.90%	1.20%	0.7%		9	-23	32
9/13/2005	0.60%	0.70%	-0.1%		11	-41	52
8/17/2005	1.00%	0.50%	0.5%		20	-14	34
7/15/2005	0.00%	0.40%	-0.4%		4	-51	55
6/14/2005	-0.60%	-0.20%	-0.4%		44	-74	118
5/17/2005	0.60%	0.40%	0.2%		10	-18	28
4/19/2005	0.70%	0.60%	0.1%		54	-6	60
3/22/2005	0.40%	0.30%	0.1%		41	0	41
2/18/2005	0.30%	0.30%	0%		36	-26	62
1/14/2005	-0.70%	-0.20%	-0.5%		28	-30	58
					30.62	-24.29	54.91 ˅

FIGURE 5.2 PPA Average Market Response for EUR/USD
Source: NewsTrader Pro | Wincorp Consulting Company | www.newstraderpro.com

the price changes for each item in the basket of goods and averaging them. The items in the basket are also weighted in accordance with their importance. CPI differentials are used in assessing price changes in the cost of living.

CPI is the most commonly used indicator for measuring inflation or deflation. Rapid increases or rapid decreases of the CPI measure that are experienced in a short period of time often indicate a period of inflation or deflation, respectively.

The Federal Reserve looks very closely at CPI and a similar report called Personal Consumption Expenditures (PCE) that adds a consumption component to the inflation indicator. The Department of Commerce's Bureau of Economic Analysis produces this report, which is otherwise known as consumption.

The PCE also measures the changes in price of consumer goods and services, but differs from the CPI in that the PCE Price Index utilizes a chain index that takes the individual's consumption into consideration with respect to changes in price, where CPI focuses on a fixed basket of goods with unchanging weightings.

Recent CPI response per currency pair is shown in Figure 5.3. CPI average market response for EUR/USD is shown in Figure 5.4.

Institute for Supply Management Manufacturing Index/Prices—ISM

The Institute for Supply Management (ISM) Manufacturing Index measures the activity level of purchasing managers in the manufacturing sector, with a reading above 50 indicating expansion. A rising trend has a positive effect on the nation's currency.

To produce the index, purchasing managers are surveyed on a number of subjects including employment, production, new orders, supplier deliveries, and inventories.

Traders watch these surveys closely because purchasing managers, by virtue of their jobs, have early access to data about their company's performance, which can be a leading indicator of overall economic performance.

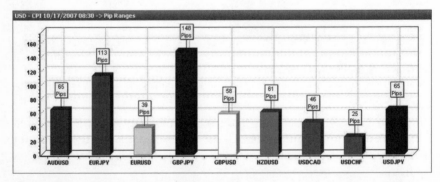

FIGURE 5.3 CPI Response per Currency Pair
Source: NewsTrader Pro | Wincorp Consulting Company | www.newstraderpro.com

(USD) CPI Price Summary 8:30 AM to 11:30 AM							

View by Symbol ▼   Select All Release Records ▼

Date	Act	Con	Diff	Revised	High	Low	Range
Symbol: EURUSD							
10/17/2007	0.3%	0.2%	0.1%	-	32	-7	39
9/19/2007	-0.1%	0.0%	-0.1%		9	-34	43
8/15/2007	0.1%	0.1%	0%		26	-19	45
7/18/2007	0.2%	0.1%	0.1%		32	-31	63
6/15/2007	0.7%	0.6%	0.1%		53	-5	58
5/15/2007	0.4%	0.5%	-0.1%		68	0	68
4/17/2007	0.6%	0.6%	0%		47	0	47
3/16/2007	0.4%	0.3%	0.1%		19	-12	31
2/21/2007	0.2%	0.1%	0.1%		0	-33	33
1/18/2007	0.5%	0.4%	0.1%		38	-26	64
12/15/2006	0.0%	0.2%	-0.2%		53	-57	110
11/16/2006	-0.5%	-0.3%	-0.2%		30	-17	47
10/18/2006	-0.5%	-0.3%	-0.2%		1	-46	47
9/15/2006	0.2%	0.2%	0%		21	-41	62
8/16/2006	0.4%	0.4%	0%		68	0	68
7/19/2006	0.2%	0.2%	0%		85	-33	118
6/14/2006	0.4%	0.4%	0%		73	-38	111
5/17/2006	0.6%	0.5%	0.1%		37	-134	171
4/19/2006	0.4%	0.4%	0%		5	-56	61
3/16/2006	0.1%	0.1%	0%		89	0	89
2/22/2006	0.70%	0.50%	0.2%		28	-4	32
1/18/2006	-0.10%	0.20%	-0.3%		30	-37	67
12/15/2005	-0.60%	-0.40%	-0.2%		7	-72	79
11/16/2005	0.20%	0.00%	0.2%		15	-39	54
10/14/2005	1.20%	0.90%	0.3%		100	-9	109
9/15/2005	0.50%	0.50%	0%		10	-34	44
8/16/2005	0.50%	0.40%	0.1%		25	-21	46
7/14/2005	0.00%	0.30%	-0.3%		50	-15	65
6/15/2005	-0.10%	0.10%	-0.2%		67	-22	89
5/18/2005	0.50%	0.40%	0.1%		41	-9	50
4/20/2005	0.60%	0.50%	0.1%		55	-53	108
3/23/2005	0.40%	0.30%	0.1%		10	-48	58
2/23/2005	0.10%	0.20%	-0.1%		32	-21	53
1/19/2005	-0.10%	0.00%	-0.1%		38	-60	98
					38.06	-30.38	68.44

FIGURE 5.4 CPI Average Market Response for EUR/USD
Source: NewsTrader Pro | Wincorp Consulting Company | www.newstraderpro.com

Manufacturing prices measures the monthly inflation experienced by manufacturing organizations when purchasing materials and services. The ISM surveys 400 firms to produce this index.

Recent ISM response per currency pair is shown in Figure 5.5. ISM average market response for EUR/USD is shown in Figure 5.6.

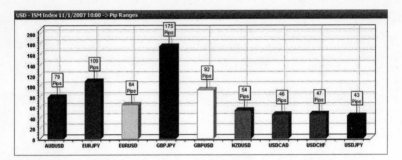

FIGURE 5.5   ISM Response per Currency Pair
Source: NewsTrader Pro | Wincorp Consulting Company | www.newstraderpro.com

(USD) ISM Index Price Summary 10:00 AM to 1:00 PM

View by Symbol ▾   Select All Release Records ▾

Date	Act	Con	Diff	Revised	High	Low	Range
⊟ Symbol: EURUSD							
11/1/2007	50.9	51.5	-0.6		54	-10	64
10/1/2007	52.0	52.5	-0.5		26	-2	28
9/4/2007	52.9	53.0	-0.1		42	-9	51
8/1/2007	53.8	55.5	-1.7		14	-28	42
7/2/2007	56.0	55.0	1		40	-4	44
6/1/2007	55.0	54.0	1		20	-36	56
5/1/2007	54.7	51.0	3.7		0	-70	70
4/2/2007	50.9	51.0	-0.1		13	-11	24
3/1/2007	52.3	50.0	2.3		0	-55	55
2/1/2007	49.3	51.5	-2.2		20	-18	38
1/3/2007	51.4	50.0	1.4		0	-71	71
12/1/2006	49.5	52.0	-2.5		57	-1	58
11/1/2006	51.2	53.0	-1.8		29	-9	38
10/2/2006	52.9	53.5	-0.6		19	-6	25
9/1/2006	54.5	54.7	-0.2		74	-1	75
8/1/2006	54.7	53.5	1.2		60	-32	92
7/3/2006	53.8	55.0	-1.2		41	-1	42
6/1/2006	54.4	55.7	-1.3		88	0	88
5/1/2006	57.3	55.0	2.3		11	-60	71
4/3/2006	55.2	57.7	-2.5		76	0	76
3/1/2006	56.7	55.5	1.2		4	-61	65
2/1/2006	54.8	55.5	-0.7		19	-24	43
1/3/2006	54.2	57.5	-3.3		49	-1	50
12/1/2005	58.1	58	0.1		18	-16	34
11/1/2005	59.1	57	2.1		22	-17	39
10/3/2005	59.4	52	7.4		0	-33	33
9/1/2005	53.6	57	-3.4		67	-1	68
8/1/2005	56.6	54.5	2.1		24	-38	62
7/1/2005	53.8	51.5	2.3		0	-123	123
6/1/2005	51.4	52	-0.6		20	-36	56
5/2/2005	53.3	55	-1.7		3	-28	31
4/1/2005	55.2	54.9	0.3		7	-135	142
3/1/2005	55.3	57	-1.7		26	-17	43
2/1/2005	56.4	57	-0.6		18	-14	32
1/3/2005	58.6	58.5	0.1		13	-33	46
					27.83	-28.6	56.43

FIGURE 5.6   ISM Average market response for EUR/USD
Source: NewsTrader Pro | Wincorp Consulting Company | www.newstraderpro.com

Retail Sales

Retail sales numbers are a total of the receipts from stores that sell durable and nondurable goods. Consumer spending accounts for 66 percent of the GDP, and as such, is an important indication of the health of the economy.

The Retail Sales report allows traders to gauge consumer confidence in the economy.

Recent retail sales response per currency pair is shown in Figure 5.7. Retail sales average response for EUR/USD is shown in Figure 5.8.

Housing

There are three different housing reports to watch on a monthly basis:

1. Housing Starts: a figure derived from the total number of new housing construction projects begun in a particular month.
2. Existing Home Sales: the sale of previously owned single-family homes. See Figure 5.9.
3. New Home Sales: the sale of newly built, never previously occupied single-family homes.

As you can see, there is a steady downward trend in existing home sales. The average was 7.09 million homes sold per month November 2005. Two years later, only 4.97 million homes sold each month. Not only is that bad news for the economy, but the rate at which sales are dropping is actually increasing. There is a similar downward trend in housing starts and new home sales.

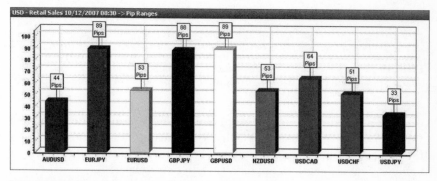

FIGURE 5.7 Retail Sales Response per Currency Pair
Source: NewsTrader Pro | Wincorp Consulting Company | www.newstraderpro.com

Date	Act	Con	Diff	Revised	High	Low	Range
Symbol: EURUSD							
10/12/2007	0.6%	0.2%	0.4%		32	-21	53
9/14/2007	0.3%	0.5%	-0.2%	0.3%	12	-36	48
8/13/2007	0.3%	0.2%	0.1%	-0.9%	10	-47	57
7/13/2007	-0.9%	0.0%	-0.9%	1.4%	36	-7	43
6/13/2007	1.4%	0.6%	0.8%	-0.2%	20	-19	39
5/11/2007	-0.2%	0.4%	-0.6%	0.7%	33	-17	50
4/16/2007	0.7%	0.4%	0.3%	0.1%	12	-7	19
3/13/2007	0.1%	0.3%	-0.2%		5	-32	37
2/14/2007	0.0%	0.3%	-0.3%	0.9%	65	-4	69
1/12/2007	0.9%	0.7%	0.2%	1.0%	59	-18	77
12/13/2006	1.0%	0.2%	0.8%	-0.4%	0	-62	62
11/14/2006	-0.2%	-0.4%	0.2%	-0.4%	27	-52	79
10/13/2006	-0.4%	0.2%	-0.6%	0.2%	16	-71	87
9/14/2006	0.2%	-0.2%	0.4%		22	-38	60
8/11/2006	1.4%	0.8%	0.6%	-0.1%	3	-58	61
7/14/2006	-0.1%	0.4%	-0.5%		14	-48	62
6/13/2006	0.1%	0.0%	0.1%	0.5%	46	-18	64
5/11/2006	0.5%	0.8%	-0.3%		107	0	107
4/13/2006	0.6%	0.5%	0.1%	-1.4%	11	-27	38
3/14/2006	-1.3%	-0.9%	-0.4%	2.3%	62	-11	73
2/14/2006	2.30%	0.90%	1.4%	0.70%	0	-43	43
1/13/2006	0.70%	1.00%	-0.3%	0.30%	47	-10	57
12/13/2005	0.30%	0.40%	-0.1%	-0.10%	11	-10	21
11/15/2005	-0.10%	-0.70%	0.6%	0.20%	37	-14	51
10/14/2005	0.20%	0.50%	-0.3%	-2.10%	100	-9	109
9/14/2005	-2.10%	-1.40%	-0.7%		6	-46	52
8/11/2005	1.80%	2.00%	-0.2%		40	-7	47
7/14/2005	1.70%	0.90%	0.8%	-0.50%	50	-15	65
6/14/2005	-0.50%	-0.20%	-0.3%	1.40%	44	-74	118
5/12/2005	1.40%	0.70%	0.7%	0.30%	0	-61	61
4/13/2005	0.30%	0.80%	-0.5%		37	-64	101
3/15/2005	0.50%	0.60%	-0.1%	-0.30%	20	-93	113
2/15/2005	-0.30%	-0.50%	0.2%	1.20%	32	-55	87
1/13/2005	1.20%	1.10%	0.1%		27	-23	50
					30.68	-32.85	63.53

FIGURE 5.8 Retail Sales Average Response for EUR/USD
Source: NewsTrader Pro | Wincorp Consulting Company | www.newstraderpro.com

It is not a surprise to see bad numbers from these reports anymore. I think the key in 2008 is to watch the average price of a home and not the number of home sold. I would not be surprised to see improving sales numbers, but if the prices are falling, I will remain bearish.

Consider how important this housing data is. If there is an increase in home purchases, this can spill over into the retail sales area because

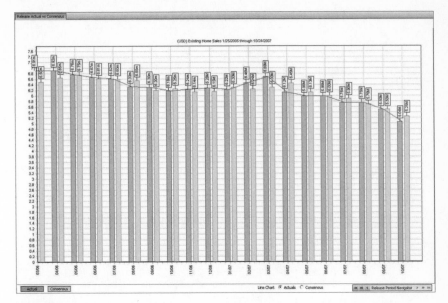

FIGURE 5.9 Existing Home Sales
Source: NewsTrader Pro | Wincorp Consulting Company | www.newstraderpro.com

people will need to purchase furniture and other durable household goods for their new homes.

Furthermore, an increase in housing starts will also affect employment levels as new construction jobs will be created to answer the need.

Trends in the housing starts figures can provide insight into the economy's relative strength.

Perhaps instead of watching three different reports, you'd rather just watch one. If there was such a report, it would be durable goods orders.

Durable Goods

This report is created by the U.S. Census Bureau and measures orders for products that will last more than three years before needing to be replaced. This typically includes large household appliances such as refrigerators and stoves, and that is why I see this report indirectly attached to the housing sector.

One note of caution, this report can include purchases made by the military, so make sure you follow the "nondefense" subcategory.

Recent durable goods response per currency pair is shown in Figure 5.10. Durable goods average response for EUR/USD is shown in Figure 5.11.

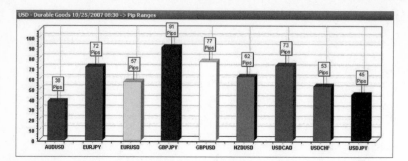

FIGURE 5.10   Durable Goods Response per Currency Pair
Source: NewsTrader Pro | Wincorp Consulting Company | www.newstraderpro.com

(USD) Durable Goods Price Summary 8:30 AM to 11:30 AM							
View by Symbol ▼ Select All Release Records ▼							
Date	Act	Con	Diff	Revised	High	Low	Range
▭ Symbol: EURUSD							
10/25/2007	-1.7%	1.5%	-3.2%	-4.9%	39	-18	57
9/26/2007	-4.9%	-3.5%	-1.4%	6.0%	4	-22	26
8/24/2007	5.9%	1.0%	4.9%	1.4%	33	-10	43
7/26/2007	1.4%	2.0%	-0.6%	-2.4%	17	-18	35
6/27/2007	-2.8%	-1.0%	-1.8%	0.6%	8	-16	24
5/24/2007	0.6%	0.9%	-0.3%	4.3%	8	-34	42
4/25/2007	3.4%	2.5%	0.9%	1.7%	21	-22	43
3/28/2007	2.5%	3.5%	-1%	-8.7%	19	-9	28
2/27/2007	-7.8%	-3.0%	-4.8%	2.9%	18	-12	30
1/26/2007	3.1%	3.5%	-0.4%	1.6%	23	-20	43
12/22/2006	1.9%	1.5%	0.4%		21	-40	61
11/28/2006	-8.3%	-5.0%	-3.3%		23	-18	41
10/26/2006	7.8%	2.3%	5.5%	-0.5%	21	-3	24
9/27/2006	-0.5%	0.4%	-0.9%	-2.5%	28	-12	40
8/24/2006	-2.4%	-0.8%	-1.6%	2.9%	10	-52	62
7/27/2006	3.1%	2.3%	0.8%	-0.2%	35	-26	61
6/23/2006	-0.3%	0.4%	-0.7%	-4.4%	33	-18	51
5/24/2006	-4.8%	-0.5%	-4.3%	6.4%	35	-122	157
4/26/2006	6.1%	1.8%	4.3%	2.7%	36	-36	72
3/24/2006	2.6%	1.3%	1.3%	-9.9%	64	-11	75
2/24/2006	-10.20%	-2.00%	-8.2%	1.30%	16	-33	49
1/26/2006	1.30%	1.00%	0.3%	4.40%	13	-22	35
12/23/2005	4.40%	1.10%	3.3%	3.40%	38	-9	47
11/29/2005	3.40%	1.50%	1.9%	-2.40%	2	-47	49
10/27/2005	-2.10%	-1.20%	-0.9%	3.40%	40	-1	41
9/28/2005	3.30%	0.70%	2.6%	-4.90%	0	-28	28
8/24/2005	-4.9	-1.50%	-3.4	2.00%	59	0	59
7/27/2005	1.40%	-1.00%	2.4%	5.50%	64	-22	86
6/24/2005	5.50%	1.50%	4%	1.90%	32	-20	52
5/25/2005	1.90%	1.30%	0.6%	-2.30%	55	-11	66
4/27/2005	-2.80%	0.30%	-3.1%	0.30%	54	0	54
3/24/2005	0.30%	0.80%	-0.5%	-1.30%	26	-26	52
2/24/2005	-0.90%	0.10%	-1%	1.10%	6	-79	85
1/27/2005	0.60%	0.70%	-0.1%	1.40%	18	-30	48
					27.03	-24.91	51.94

FIGURE 5.11   Durable Goods Average Response for EUR/USD
Source: NewsTrader Pro | Wincorp Consulting Company | www.newstraderpro.com

Nonfarm Payrolls—NFP

This report is researched and produced by the U.S. Bureau of Labor Statistics to identify the total number of paid workers in the U.S. The contributions of approximately 80 percent of all workers are calculated in the U.S. GDP, which excludes the following sectors:

- General government employees.
- Private household employees.
- Employees of nonprofit organizations.
- Farm employees.

The report also includes estimations on the average work week and average weekly earnings of the nonfarm employees.

Recent NFP response per currency pair is shown in Figure 5.12. NFP average market response for EUR/USD is shown in Figure 5.13.

Gross Domestic Product—GDP

This report measures the pace of the economy's growth. GDP is the sum total worth of all goods and services irrespective of sales being complete or items placed in inventories within a given period of time.

GDP is seen as an overall barometer of the economy as a whole. Since the end of the second world war, the United States has been in a continuous growing cycle with expansion phases being longer than the contraction phases.

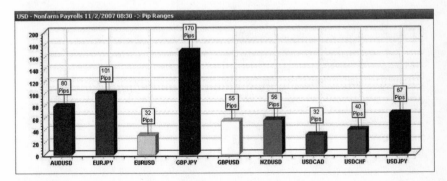

FIGURE 5.12 NFP Response per Currency Pair
Source: NewsTrader Pro | Wincorp Consulting Company | www.newstraderpro.com

The official results come out quarterly, (every three months). GDP is subject to wild variations and revisions and is often averaged out on a yearly basis. For example:

	Quarterly Results
August 2007:	4.0%
May 2007:	0.6%
February 2007:	2.2%

(USD) Nonfarm Payrolls Price Summary 8:30 AM to 11:30 AM

View by Symbol ▼ Select All Release Records ▼

Date	Act	Con	Diff	Revised	High	Low	Range
Symbol: EURUSD							
11/2/2007	166K	80K	86k	110K	13	-19	32
10/5/2007	110K	100K	10k		29	-94	123
9/7/2007	-4K	110K	-114k	92K	101	0	101
8/3/2007	92K	135K	-43k	132K	84	0	84
7/6/2007	132K	125K	7k	157K	40	-32	72
6/1/2007	157K	135K	22k	88K	25	-44	69
5/4/2007	88K	100K	-12k	180k	58	0	58
4/6/2007	180k	135K	45k	97k	0	-50	50
3/9/2007	97K	100K	-3k	111K	0	-60	60
2/2/2007	111K	150K	-39k	167K	26	-72	98
1/5/2007	167K	100K	67k	132K	0	-86	86
12/8/2006	132K	105K	27k	92K	93	-33	126
11/3/2006	92k	125k	-33k	51k	0	-78	78
10/6/2006	51k	120k	-69k	128k	42	-99	141
9/1/2006	128k	125k	3k	113k	7	-47	54
8/4/2006	113k	145k	-32k		92	0	92
7/7/2006	121k	175k	-54k	75k	44	-6	50
6/2/2006	75k	170k	-95k	138k	102	0	102
5/5/2006	138k	200k	-62k	211k	78	0	78
4/7/2006	211k	190k	21k	243k	38	-74	112
3/10/2006	243k	210k	33k	193k	0	-60	60
2/3/2006	193k	250k	-57k	108k	23	-91	114
1/6/2006	108k	200k	-92k	215k	86	-4	90
12/2/2005	215k	210k	5k	56k	48	-39	87
11/4/2005	56k	100k	-44k	-35k	67	-121	188
10/7/2005	-35k	-150k	115k	169k	0	-48	48
9/2/2005	169k	190k	-21k	207k	17	-54	71
8/5/2005	207k	180k	27k	146k	10	-66	76
7/8/2005	146k	195k	-49k	78k	85	-27	112
6/3/2005	78k	175k	-97k		45	-60	105
5/6/2005	274k	175k	99k	110k	0	-138	138
4/1/2005	110k	220k	-110k	262k	93	-92	185
3/4/2005	262k	225k	37k	146k	133	-19	152
2/4/2005	146k	200k	-54k	157k	75	-54	129
1/7/2005	157k	175k	-18k	112k	62	-137	199
					46.17	-51.54	97.71

FIGURE 5.13 NFP Average Market Response for EUR/USD
Source: NewsTrader Pro | Wincorp Consulting Company | www.newstraderpro.com

GDP attempts to represent everything in the economy. It is the broadest measure of aggregate economic activity from every sector. Bernard Baumohl, former *Time* magazine senior economics reporter once wrote:

> "With more people working, total household income goes up. This encourages Americans to spend more on goods and services. As consumer spending accelerates, companies will be inclined to speed up their own production and hire additional workers ... which in turn brings in more for households. ... Rinse and repeat."
> —Bernard Baumohl, *The Secrets of Economic Indicators: Hidden Clues to Future Economic Trends and Investment Opportunities*

Recent GDP response per currency pair is shown in Figure 5.14. GDP (preliminary) average response for EUR/USD is shown in Figure 5.15.

THE FEDERAL RESERVE SYSTEM

The Fed is the gatekeeper of the U.S. economy. It is the bank of the U.S. government and, as such, it regulates the nation's financial institutions. The Fed watches over the world's largest economy and is, therefore, one of the most powerful organizations on earth. (Investopedia. com)

As an investor, it is essential to acquire a basic knowledge of the Federal Reserve System. The Fed dictates economic and monetary policies that have profound impacts on individuals in the U.S. and around the world.

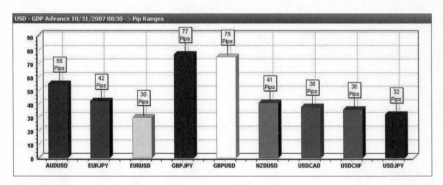

FIGURE 5.14 GDP Response per Currency Pair
Source: NewsTrader Pro | Wincorp Consulting Company | www.newstraderpro.com

(USD) GDP Preliminary Price Summary 8:30 AM to 11:30 AM							
View by Symbol ▼	Select All Release Records		▼				
Date	Act	Con	Diff	Revised	High	Low	Range
⊟ Symbol: EURUSD							
8/30/2007	4.0%	4.1%	-0.1%		40	-8	48
5/31/2007	0.6%	0.8%	-0.2%		10	-28	38
2/28/2007	2.2%	2.3%	-0.1%		8	-31	39
11/29/2006	2.2%	1.8%	0.4%		36	-9	45
8/30/2006	2.9%	3.0%	-0.1%		16	-14	30
5/25/2006	5.30%	5.80%	-0.5%		37	-8	45
2/28/2006	1.60%	1.60%	0%		53	-5	58
11/30/2005	4.30%	4.00%	0.3%		24	-23	47
8/31/2005	3.30%	3.40%	-0.1%		107	0	107
5/26/2005	3.50%	3.60%	-0.1%		17	-23	40
2/25/2005	3.80%	3.70%	0.1%		42	-4	46
					35.45	-13.91	49.36

FIGURE 5.15 GDP (Preliminary) Average Response for EUR/USD
Source: NewsTrader Pro | Wincorp Consulting Company | www.newstraderpro.com

The Fed's Mission

The Federal Reserve System is the central bank of the United States. It was created back in 1913 to provide the nation with a more stable monetary economy. Before the establishment of the Fed, Americans faced a brutal boom-and-bust financial system.

Today, the Federal Reserve's duties fall into three general areas:

1. Influencing the monetary and credit conditions to establish a healthy economy. Such actions reduce systemic risk of the previous boom-and-bust cycles.
2. Regulating the banking system to protect the American consumer.
3. Providing financial services to the U.S. government, foreign countries, and acting as the "bank for banks."

Governors vs. Presidents

The Fed comprises seven governors located in the nation's capital. It also has 12 reserve banks strategically located in key areas of the country in order to keep tabs on the local economy (see Figure 5.16). The idea is that each bank represents a regional economy and vote with that region's best interests in mind.

For example, Denver may have a recessionary environment and Detroit may have a depression environment. This could induce a moderate

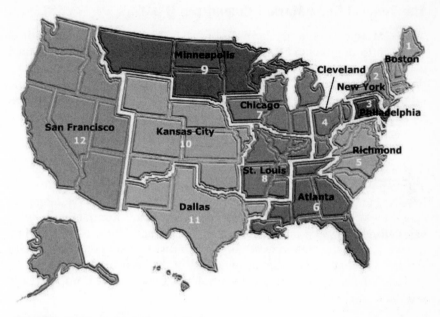

FIGURE 5.16 Federal Reserve Map
Source: The Federal Reserve (www.federalreserve.gov)

and aggressive vote, respectively, by the two Fed members representing those areas.

How the Fed Works

Remember, the overall responsibility of the Fed is to ensure a healthy and balanced economy.

One way it does this is to insure we have a banking system that can be trusted. Before the Fed was created, banks often went bust because they didn't have enough cash on deposit; it was all loaned out. So today, the Federal Reserve regulates minimum bank deposits and makes short-term loans to banks that need help meeting these requirements. The Fed also ensures these banks follow federal laws, such as fair lending practices.

The other way the Fed meets its overall objective is through its open market operations, adding and subtracting money supply in the economy. It's called "open market" because money adjustments are made via the public bond and treasury market. To oversee these monetary actions, the Fed formed the Federal Open Market Committee.

The Federal Open Market Committee (FOMC)

The FOMC meets on a regular basis and, believe it or not, these meetings are open to the public. I think I will take a trip to Washington, D.C., and catch a meeting sometime. I always thought money was a more interesting discussion than politics. However, the committee's key meetings to decide on policy changes are closed to the public with the decisions announced via press release, such as a change in interest rates.

Talking with Government

The Fed and therefore the FOMC are not government agencies, yet they have a dramatic impact on the U.S. economy. Federal Reserve members spend most of their time gathering information and formulating a strategy before they take any action (just like a trade plan). Although they are not part of the government, they consult with members of the Senate Finance Committee, such as the Secretary of the Treasury Henry Paulson, Jr. The Fed also meets with other central banks such as the European Central Bank and the Bank of Japan.

Talking with Business

Each member bank of the Fed interviews business leaders in its region and formulates its own bias on the economy. They compile this information and send it the Fed chairman. Federal Reserve staffers compile the report, and create what's called the "Beige Book." It got its name because the cover was beige in color. Brilliant, eh?

FOMC Meetings

So with business, government, and international trading partners all surveyed, the FOMC meet to discuss a plan of action. The board members hold a two-day meeting and vote on interest rate policy, after which they announce their decision:

1. Raise interest rates.
2. Lower interest rates.
3. Leave interest rates unchanged.

A couple of weeks later, the minutes from this meeting and the results of the board's votes are released to the public.

Fed Cycle

Figure 5.17 shows the Fed's rate policy cycle in a nutshell.

SUMMARY

Analysis of fundamental economic data to derive central bank policy will certainly help you develop a bullish or bearish bias toward any currency you choose to study. Your forex trading should go with the money flow and interest rates create long-term trends.

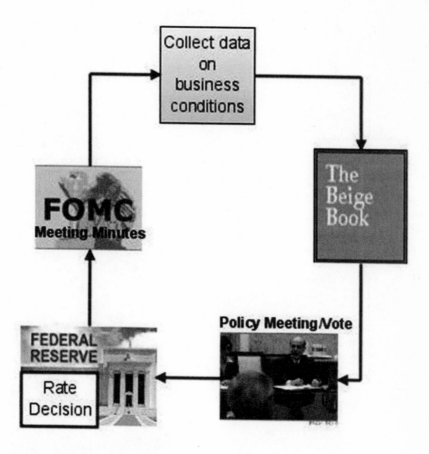

FIGURE 5.17 The FED Cycle
Source: The Federal Reserve (www.federalreserve.gov)

However, interest rates are not the only thing that can impact global money flow. Commodities that are consumed by economies around the world also act like money magnets. The two I love to trade via the forex market are oil and gold. Currency traders simply buy and sell money. In my humble opinion oil *is* money. Gold *is* money. Chapter 6 will explore how you can use moves in the commodities market to find opportunities to trade the currency market.

Commodity Correlations

M oney flows to high interest rates because investors will receive a higher return for their investment of cash. However, money also flows based on how people spend their money.

Demand for commodities, such as gold, oil, and stocks, will change the value of a currency. Why? If you wanted to buy gold, you would do so with the local currency of the producer. Therefore, you would sell your currency to buy the local currency and then trade it for gold.

If your gold was mined in South Africa, then you'd need to buy South African (ZAR) rand first, then trade your ZAR for gold. If a lot of people did this, prices for gold and prices for rand would rise with demand.

This is true for all commodities. If you wanted to buy a stock listed in the German equities market, the DAX, you'd need to buy EUR first. Fairly logical, eh? However, it is important to know what to buy or sell when you see commodities prices rise and fall. FX Bootcamp has researched the correlation between commodities prices and currency values in 2007, called intermarket analysis, and in this chapter I will show you what currencies to trade when oil, gold, and stock markets are moving.

COMMODITY CORRELATION: OIL

Petroleum, also known as crude oil, is a major driver of the global economy. It's best known as, and used mostly (by volume) for producing, the gasoline that powers most cars. Less well known to many, however, is oil's use in creating the natural gas that heats your home, the asphalt you drive on, all plastics, and food-protecting pesticides.

Because oil is used in so many ways, growing economies usually demand a lot of it. The emergence of China and India as economic powers has dramatically changed the global oil demand equation. As new businesses have formed and grown in those countries, and increasing numbers of their populations have attained financial affluence, the Far East has become a growing sponge for oil.

My recent visit to China included a speech in Chengdu, near the Tibetan border. Even way out there, the city was modern, business was booming, and there were cars everywhere. Beijing was just the same; they need energy!

Fortunately, as a forex trader you can profit from the movement in oil prices by trading the Canadian dollar.

Loonie for Oil

In 2006, Canada was the 15th largest exporter of oil, as shown in Table 6.1.

Canada's position in the world oil rankings seems poised for a boost in the coming years. As of January 2007, Canada's proven oil reserves were estimated at 179.2 billion barrels, ranking the country second only to Saudi Arabia (Energy Information Administration (EIA) of the U.S. Department of Energy International Energy Outlook 2007).

TABLE 6.1 Top World Oil Net Exporters, 2006 (Thousand barrels per day)

Rank	Country	Net Exports
1	Saudi Arabia	8,651
2	Russia	6,565
3	Norway	2,542
4	Iran	2,519
5	United Arab Emirates	2,515
6	Venezuela	2,203
7	Kuwait	2,150
8	Nigeria	2,146
9	Algeria	1,847
10	Mexico	1,676
11	Libya	1,525
12	Iraq	1,438
13	Angola	1,363
14	Kazakhstan	1,114
15	Canada	1,071

Source: Energy Information Administration (EIA), U.S. Dept. of Energy

More than 95 percent of these reserves consist of oil sands deposits in the Canadian province of Alberta. Analysts have estimated that an oil price of at least $40 per barrel is required to make production from the Alberta oil sands profitable (EIA Country Analysis Brief: Canada., 2007).

With oil prices reaching $135 per barrel in May 2008, oil sands production has become profitable. For example, Royal Dutch Shell stated in its 2006 annual report that its Canadian oil sands unit earned an after-tax profit nearly double the amount of its worldwide profit on conventional crude. As a result, companies like Royal Dutch Shell are making massive investments in oil sands projects (Carl Mortished, "Shell Rakes in Profits from Canadian Oil Sands Unit," *The Times*, July 27, 2007, http://business.timesonline.co.uk/tol/business/industry_sectors/natural_resources/article2148631.ece).

With oil prices rising in a world likely to exhibit a growing appetite for oil, a country like Canada, sitting on massive oil reserves, stands to reap tremendous economic benefits. Fundamentally speaking that means that the Canadian dollar should gain strength as oil prices rise.

Over the 12 months from October 2006 through September 2007, there is a −0.92 correlation coefficient between USD/CAD with West Texas Intermediate (WTI) spot oil prices. That simply means when oil goes up, USD/CAD has a very strong tendency to go down as the Canadian dollar increases in value.

The opposite scenario also applies. When oil goes down, USD/CAD tends to go up. In a statistical sense, approximately 84 percent of USD/CAD price movement is explained by the variance in oil prices. Note that this does not tell us that oil prices are the sole cause for changes in the exchange rate of U.S. and Canadian dollars, only that the two variables move in tandem.

Until now, you've probably winced each time you fill up your car's gas tank after gas prices have risen. If you learn to profitably trade the USD/CAD currency pair, you may find yourself cheering each time oil prices rise. The guy next to you is crying because gas prices are 23 cents higher. You are smiling ear to ear because you are shorting the USD/CAD. It can be a beautiful thing.

COMMODITY CORRELATION: GOLD

The supply of gold in the world marketplace has generally not kept pace with demand. On the supply side, gold producers have not invested in locating new mines in recent years. Demand for both jewelry and investment, however, is increasing, especially as economic growth in China and India has led consumers in those countries to attain greater disposable income.

According to the National Mining Association,

"Gold's superior electrical conductivity, its malleability, and its resistance to corrosion have made it vital to the manufacture of components used in a wide range of electronic products and equipment, including computers, telephones, cellular phones, and home appliances.

Gold has extraordinarily high reflective powers that are relied upon in the shielding that protects spacecrafts and satellites from solar radiation and in industrial and medical lasers that use gold-coated reflectors to focus light energy. And because gold is biologically inactive, it has become a vital tool for medical research and is even used in the direct treatment of arthritis and other intractable diseases." (www.nma.org/about_us/publications/pub_gold_uses.asp)

Obviously there is high demand for gold for use in jewelry, but there is also a huge need for the metal in the dentist industry. According to *Discover* magazine, gold was first used by early dentists to attach fake teeth back in the seventh century B.C. On an annual basis, as much as 70 tons of gold has been used just by the dental industry alone.

All this aside, there is also a lingering perception in the market that gold is a safe haven investment and this greatly adds to the yellow metal's allure.

As the world's third largest producer of gold, Australia stands to benefit from a rise in gold prices. In fact, exports of gold from Australia grew by 55 percent to $10.6 billion in 2006 (Australian Department of Foreign Affairs and Trade, http://www.dfat.gov.au/toos/archive/2007/trade2007.pdf).

During the 12 months from October 2006 through September 2007, there is a 0.78 correlation coefficient between AUD/USD and gold prices. As a result, increases in gold price usually result in a rising Aussie dollar, and a drop in the AUD/USD is usually preceded by a decline in gold prices. It's not a perfect correlation, but with 78 percent accuracy, it shouldn't be ignored.

COMMODITY CORRELATION: EQUITIES

Okay, stocks are not a commodity, but they can correlate well with the currency markets and must not be overlooked.

At FX Bootcamp, we don't focus on specific stocks, just the major stock indexes around the world. Japan's Nikkei, Germany's DAX, the United Kingdom's FTSE and the United States' S&P 500 are very important to forex and we watch them along with our currencies. Why not? Money flows into and out of the markets, and this global money flow impacts the value of money.

A stock index is simply a broad basket of stocks listed on the exchange. As the general market rises, it is obviously attracting buyers of stocks listed on the exchange and tracked with the index. As foreign money pours into the market, it is converted into the local currency. As the market falls, investors are cashing out and want their local currency back. This is how the stock markets directly impact currency values.

Does that mean if the Nikkei is rising you should buy JPY or if the DAX falls you should short EUR? Perhaps, but wouldn't it be easier to have a one-trade-fits-all option? You may have one. It is an indirect relationship, but FX Bootcamp statistics show it is still an effective alternative.

Trading the EUR/JPY is a measure of risk tolerance by traders around the globe. It moves very closely with the major stock indexes, not because currency is flowing in and out of each of the stock markets, but because of traders' willingness to get into or out of the markets in general.

Therefore, if investors feel confident that the markets are rising around the world, they begin to invest and this increases their willingness to put their money on the line. In such cases, most of the time the EUR/JPY rises, too. If investors are not confident and are taking money out of the markets, most of the time the EUR/JPY falls. Not always, but most of the time.

For example, according to data provided by MetaTrader 4, the EUR/JPY had a high correlation coefficient with the global stock indexes in 2007. So, if you are trading the European and U.S. forex trading sessions, it would be good to keep a close eye on the DAX and S&P 500 as they will move with the forex market.

European Session: DUMMUY	EUR/JPY	GBP/JPY
DAX	87%	46%
U.S. Session:		
S&P 500	88%	64%

Note, not all markets are created equal, although the EUR/JPY correlation coefficient is always above 0.80, the GBP/JPY is only 52 percent correlated with the Dow and 36 percent correlated with NASDAQ.

So as you can see, there is a relationship with DAX and S&P that could be beneficial to your trading. If you are watching the financial television news stations, reading the newspapers, or watching the stock charts along with your currencies charts, you can take advantage of equities moves and trade the EUR/JPY and get a very similar result. What does a high correlation look like on the charts? In reviewing Figures 6.1 and 6.2, you will notice that they seem to have had a fairly similar year.

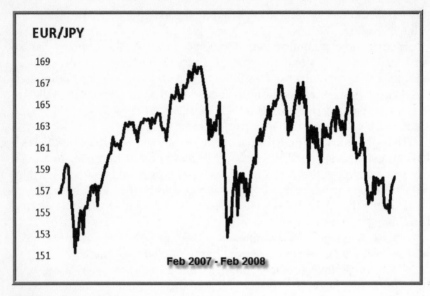

FIGURE 6.1   EUR/JPY
Source: FX Bootcamp, LLC (www.fxbootcamp.com)

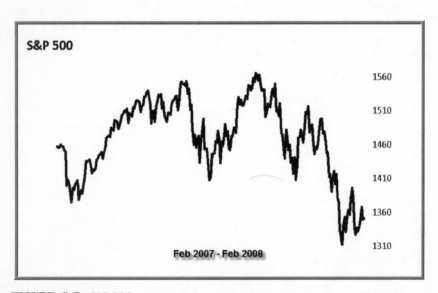

FIGURE 6.2   S&P 500
Source: FX Bootcamp, LLC (www.fxbootcamp.com)

TRADING COMMODITIES

You don't need to watch the commodities market minute by minute, although you can if you wish. Generally speaking, if gold prices are rising, the AUD may rise, too. If oil prices are rising, CAD may rise, too. Each economy has a high percentage of its GDP tied to these commodities, respectively.

However, please remember that these are fundamentals and do not affect the value of the currency in real time. You are looking for trends. All you need to do is read the newspaper and keep abreast of oil and gold prices.

At FX Bootcamp, every Wednesday we trade the Department of Energy's oil inventory data. It tells you how much oil we have stored up for the future. Believe it or not, we usually only have enough saved to last a few weeks at current demand. So, for example, if we see that inventories are low, assuming demand is constant, then prices will rise. If prices rise, we may have an opportunity to go short the USD/CAD or long CAD/JPY. It's not like a typical economics report that moves the market instantly. But it does move the market.

Wednesdays may be my favorite trading day and the oil inventories CAD trade is definitely part of it.

SUMMARY

Money flows based on supply and demand. It may be a supply and demand for return on investment, such as interest rates. It can also be supply and demand for a commodity such as wheat (food for humans), soy beans (food for humans or feed for animals), corn (food, feed and energy if used for ethanol), gold (inflationary hedge, jewelery, dentistry, and electronics), oil (power, gasoline, fertilizer, plastics, and fabrics) and such.

Many economies have some of the resources they need, but none have all of them. They reach outside of their borders for the commodities they need: to Canada for oil, to Australia for gold, to the United States for corn, to Brazil for soy beans, for example. When lack of supply increases demand it will drive up the value of the currency for the economy, which exports the commodity, because the commodity is purchased with the local currency. Supply and demand at its best!

So where do you start as a new forex trader? I suggest the USD.

CHAPTER 7

Greenback Guru: Why You Should Specialize in Trading U.S. Dollars

I f you are a currency trader, and focus on trading the *major* currency pairs—EUR/USD, GBP/USD, USD/CHF, and USD/JPY—then you should consider yourself a specialist. Yes, it's true! You are a specialist in the U.S. dollar—a "greenback guru" so to speak.

Each currency pair obviously comprises two currencies. If you are long the GBP/USD, then you are actually buying pounds and selling dollars. If you are short the USD/JPY, then you are actually selling dollars and buying yen.

In each of the major currency pairs, the USD is a part of the equation. This means if you study and understand the fundamentals of the U.S. dollar, the U.S. economy, and the inner workings of the U.S. Federal Reserve System, then you've done most of the work needed to prepare to trade any of the four major currency pairs.

The so-called majors are the most liquid and widely traded currency pairs in the world. Trades involving the majors make up the vast majority of total forex trading.

Think about it. If the USD is half of every major currency pair, and the majors comprise most of the entire forex market, then your focus on understanding what drives the USD will have a *huge* impact on nearly all of your future trade plans.

There is also a wonderful benefit of specializing in trading the USD. The U.S. dollar, since the end of World War II, has been the reserve currency of the world. What does that mean? It means that the fate of the USD has a much larger impact on the forex market than any other currency.

TABLE 7.1 Currency Composition of the World's Forex Reserves

Currency	% of total
USD	66.3%
EUR	24.8%
GBP	4.0%
JPY	3.4%

Source: Currency Composition of Official Foreign Exchange Reserves (www.imf.org)

As of the start of 2006, according to the International Monetary Fund (IMF), the combined currency composition of the world's identified official foreign exchange reserves was as shown in Table 7.1.

This should illustrate that virtually every investor, business, and central bank pays close attention to the value of the USD. They care because they own it.

WHAT'S YOUR USD BIAS?

The only thing you need to do is determine your bias (if the U.S. dollar is likely to strengthen or weaken, in your opinion), then apply this bias to the various major currency pairs.

Notice what side of the equation the USD is in the currency pair. When you buy a currency pair, you are buying the first currency and selling the other.

For example, if your bias is for the U.S. dollar to strengthen, then you would want to buy USD. Table 7.2 is a list of the kind of trade you would enter in each of the four major currency pairs.

TABLE 7.2 Trading the Four Major Currency Pairs

Pair	Buy or Sell
USD/CHF	Buy
USD/JPY	Buy
EUR/USD	Sell
GBP/USD	Sell

Source: FX Bootcamp, LLC (www.fxbootcamp.com)

In all cases, you are *long* the USD and *short* the other currency in the pair. One bias, four trades!

This is generally true, but each currency pair will react differently to the USD. That's because each local currency pair has its own strengths and weaknesses—its own value. For example, if the EUR is also strengthening it would move less with the USD strengthening than the JPY if the yen was weakening.

Here's a trade trick you can try. Let's say you can only afford to place one mini lot trade and you have a bearish bias for the USD. You can consider going long the GBP/USD or EUR/USD—but which currency pair do you trade? Take a look at the EUR/GBP. Which is stronger, the EUR or the GBP? Trade the stronger currency on the majors using your bias for the USD. If EUR/GBP is down, go long on GBP/USD. Cool, eh?

Generally speaking, however, the majors all move predictably in one direction or the other in relation to the strength or weakness of the USD.

How often is this true? Not 100 percent of the time, but most of the time.

CURRENCY CORRELATION COEFFICIENT

You should always include an evaluation of currency correlation for the majors in every trade plan that you create. The correlation between currency pairs *can* change at any time, even for pairs, which are normally 95 percent-plus correlated.

Correlation is determined by what is known as the correlation coefficient, which ranges between −1 and +1. Table 7.3 explains the meaning behind that number.

TABLE 7.3 Correlation Coefficient

Type of Correlation	Correlation Coefficient	Interpretation
Perfect positive correlation	+1	As one pair moves, either up or down, the other pair will move in the same direction
Perfect negative correlation	−1	If one pair moves, either up or down, the other pair will move in the opposite direction
Zero correlation	0	The two pairs move independently of one another; there is no relationship between movement of one pair and the other

Source: FX Bootcamp, LLC (www.fxbootcamp.com)

TRADING CURRENCY CORRELATION

Say, for example, that you've located the following data on currency correlation coefficients (see Table 7.4) and determined the following:

- The GBP/USD moved the same as the EUR/USD 68 percent of the time.
- USD/CHF moved in the opposite direction of the EUR/USD 97.5 percent of the time.

Armed with this kind of information, you can avoid entering two different positions that would likely cancel each other out.

By knowing that EUR/USD and USD/CHF move in opposite directions most of the time, you would conclude that having an open long trade in EUR/USD, while also being in a long USD/CHF trade, is the same as having virtually no position at all. The two trades would effectively cancel each other out, due to the negative correlation exhibited by these two pairs.

In other words, when your long EUR/USD position moves up in price, your USD/CHF long will be going down by nearly the same amount, resulting in a pretty pointless trade at double the spread cost.

Instead, the savvy trader, understanding this negative correlation, would enter both a long EUR/USD position and a short USD/CHF position—basically, shorting the USD in two different trades. However, you are diversifying your USD bearish investment.

More importantly, you can make trade entry and exit decisions based on currency correlation. Say, for example, the GBP/USD starts showing some volatility and approaches a resistance level. While you anticipate entering a long trade on a breakout, you notice that the other three major currency pairs are not moving in proportion to the pound's move. In other words, the EUR/USD is not moving up, the USD/CHF is not moving down, and the USD/JPY is not moving down. This is a clue that the pound's move might be driven by, say, news on the British economy, or a major corporate merger involving a U.K.-based company.

Knowing that this move is pound-driven and not USD-driven, you can shift your focus to either:

1. Making a GBP/USD trade with reduced risk (involving fewer mini-lots), or
2. Ignoring the GBP's move, and waiting for a later opportunity that involves simultaneous, correlated moves of all major pairs.

Consider another scenario: You've just entered a short EUR/USD trade, and you're scanning for clues as to whether the pair will either proceed down toward your profit target or go against you and cause you to exit with a small loss.

TABLE 7.4 Correlation Coefficients

	EURUSD	GBPUSD	USDCHF	USDJPY	EURGBP	EURCHF	EURJPY	GBPCHF	GBPJPY
EURUSD	1.00	−0.27	−0.98	−0.94	0.96	−0.69	−0.30	−0.94	−0.89
GBPUSD		1.00	0.34	0.37	−0.53	0.51	0.44	0.55	0.57
USDCHF			1.00	0.97	−0.96	0.81	0.44	0.97	0.94
USDJPY				1.00	−0.93	0.82	0.61	0.95	0.97
EURGBP					1.00	−0.75	−0.39	−0.99	−0.95
EURCHF						1.00	0.73	0.84	0.85
EURJPY							1.00	0.50	0.65
GBPCHF								1.00	0.98
GBPJPY									1.00

Based on daily closing prices from 05/28/2007 through 05/23/2008.
Source: FX Bootcamp, LLC (www.fxbootcamp.com)

Your EUR/USD trade has broken the S1 support pivot level and appears headed for M1. However, the pound has just paused at its own S1 pivot level and is showing signs of reversing to the upside.

In this kind of situation, currency correlation might tell you that the pound needs to break through its S1 before the euro can reach M1. If the pound does break its S1 level, then you're probably poised to exit your short euro trade at M1 with a profit. If the pound reverses and heads back to the upside, then you start watching the indicators that will tell you when to exit the trade (according to your trade plan) before incurring a significant loss.

TRADING A BASKET OF CURRENCIES

As you mature in your forex training, you may eventually choose to diversify your risk by trading a so-called "basket" of all four majors based on one correlated, simultaneous movement of the USD.

Let's say you are currently trading four lots on the EUR/USD. If you are right, you'll be totally right. However, if you're wrong, you'll be totally wrong.

With currency correlation, you spread the risk around so that you are only *mostly* right or wrong. Most of the time, the majors are moving in correlation, just at different speeds (see Table 7.5). So if you only bought EUR/USD and it moved slowly upward while the GBP/USD skyrockets, you were right in your USD analysis, you just bet on the wrong horse.

By putting a single lot on each of the major currency pairs based on their correlation, you are really betting on all the horses. Each of the trades will profit (or lose) differently, but you'll be mostly right (or wrong). You don't have to worry about how right or wrong. All you have to worry about is direction: up or down.

TABLE 7.5 Correlation Coefficients

	EURUSD	USDJPY	GBPUSD	USDCHF	USDCAD	AUDUSD
EURUSD	1.00	−0.94	−0.27	−0.98	−0.57	0.87
USDJPY		1.00	0.37	0.97	0.48	−0.72
GBPUSD			1.00	0.34	−0.29	−0.13
USDCHF				1.00	0.49	−0.82
USDCAD					1.00	−0.69
AUDUSD						1.00

Based on daily closing prices from 05/28/2007 through 05/23/2008.
Source: FX Bootcamp, LLC (www.fxbootcamp.com)

So, for example, if you felt the USD was going to fall, you would place a lot on each of the major currencies, in contrast to placing four lots on just one pair. With this strategy, your basket of majors would look like Table 7.6.

PETRODOLLARS

Need yet another reason to focus on the USD? Let me introduce you to the petrodollar.

Did you know that all oil purchases from OPEC are paid for in U.S. dollars? For example, if South Korea wants to buy oil from Saudi Arabia, it has to sell its local currency and buy U.S. dollars, then use those dollars to buy oil from OPEC. If Norway wants to buy oil, it has the sell its local currency and buy U.S. dollars.

Any country that buys oil from OPEC, must do so using petrodollars. A lot of countries need more oil than they can produce, and a lot of countries buy their oil from OPEC. That means a *lot* of oil purchases and a lot of USD being bought just for that purpose!

Petrodollars Defined

Here's the complete definition provided by Investopedia:

Petrodollars: The money that oil exporters receive from selling oil and then deposit into Western banks. Petrodollars are also known as petrocurrency.

In other words, petrodollars is a term used to define money that oil-producing Middle Eastern countries and members of OPEC receive as revenue from Western nations, then put back into those same nations' banks.

For example, if Saudi Arabia were to receive money from the U.S. for oil and it then put the money into a U.S. bank, that deposited money is referred to as petrodollars.

TABLE 7.6 Trading the Four Major Currency Pairs When USD Is Falling

Pair	Buy or Sell
USD/CHF	Sell
USD/JPY	Sell
EUR/USD	Buy
GBP/USD	Buy

Source: FX Bootcamp, LLC (www.fxbootcamp.com)

YET ANOTHER REASON

Now you have several reasons you should consider becoming a specialist in trading the U.S. dollar:

1. The currency pairs involving USD comprise about 90 percent of all forex trades.
2. The USD is the reserve currency of the world.
3. The USD is bought as petrodollars by governments around the world for their energy needs.
4. All of these greatly increase demand for the USD.

The USD is unique indeed! For forex traders, there is no better currency in which to specialize. These characteristics are advantageous to the currency, as they have built-in demand that props up its value.

However, will this bullish system of petrodollars continue forever for the USD? Only time will tell. But it is doubtful. In current news there are rumors that Saudi Arabia, worried about the depreciating dollar, will drop its peg to the USD and also start accepting payment for its oil in euros, as well as USD. That will be bearish for the USD.

SUMMARY

As you can see, the USD is a very unique currency. It has many advantages and characteristics that other currencies do not have. It's a great currency to start your forex career with. Once you develop skills trading the majors by way of your USD bias, you may begin to branch out into other pairs, but not until you have a trade record of success with the majors.

You must first become a great currency analyst who has a strong understanding of technical and fundamental analysis. You must be an expert in reading your charts and know how money flows around the globe. From this, you can begin to refine your skills as a trader—an entirely different matter.

How many times has your analysis been correct, but you still lost money trading forex? Many traders admit it happens all the time. The difference between solid analysis and profitably trading is knowing the rules of engagement—knowing how to implement your analysis by creating a trade plan.

PART TWO SUMMARY

To recap, the key takeaways for Part Two are as follows:

- Strategy is creating a fundamental bias based on the study of economies.
- Economic data points to inflation.
- High interest rates attract money to them.
- Foreign investors must buy the local currency of that country.
- This drives up the demand and increases the valuation of the currency.
- Low valuation is good for exporters, bad for importers.
- Wide interest rate differentials attract arbitrage traders.
- Carry traders borrow cheap money and invest it in higher yielding assets.
- Carry trade risk comes from price volatility.
- Fundamentals can reverse trends and increase volatility.
- As a trader it is important to track economic trends like central bankers do.
- Central banks manage and maintain healthy economies and indirectly currency valuations.
- They control money supply and costs.
- Exporting economies like low valuations.
- Importing economies like high valuations.
- Low interest rates tend to lower valuations.
- High interest rates tend to raise valuations.
- Currency valuations tend to correlate directly or inversely with each other.
- USD is the reserve currency of the world in all of the major currency pairs and is used by other economies to buy oil.
- These are good reasons for new traders to specialize in trading USD.
- Currencies also correlate with commodities such as gold, oil, and stock indexes.
- Oil prices correlate with CAD.
- Gold prices correlate with AUD.
- Stock prices correlate with EUR/JPY.

Rules of Engagement

How to Plan Your Trades and Trade Your Plans

In Part Three, you will learn how to plan your trades. Planning your trades in advance is the secret to success in forex. It will put you in and take you out of trades, but more importantly, it will keep you out of trades, and undoubtedly a lot of the trades you will miss would have been bad trades.

Trade plans allow you to focus your energy on analysis and focus your trading on implementing your analysis. Anyone can pull the trigger. That is the easy part.

Traders who desire to be successful in the long run will need to develop skills that are repeatable, skills they can use every day. Those skills are gathering intelligence and formulating a strategy.

In Part Three, you will learn:

- How to align price, market, and trend.
- How to find support and resistance.
- How to trade S&R role reversals.
- How to use lagging indicators to enter trades.
- How to use leading indicators to exit trades.
- How to get a second chance on your trades.

- How to manage news trading.
- How to use pivot points.
- How to use Fibonacci studies.
- How to manage money.
- How to manage trades.
- How to manage a loss.
- When to not pull the trigger.
- How to take control of your trading.

WHAT'S THE TIME?

Your fundamental bias is created from analysis of economic data and its impact on an economy's interest rates. A trade plan will take that bias and combine it with technical analysis.

If the currency is moving in the direction of your fundamental bias, you may consider long-term trades. This is because price is moving in the direction you want it to, based on your analysis. Because currencies trend so well, an ideal trade would keep you in the trend for a long period of time.

The pips will be easy. All you would have to do is log into your account once a day or once a week and move your stop loss to protect more profit. It would take very little time to do so. As icing on the cake, many currency pairs will also pay you interest on top of your pips. Long-term trades with stop losses above breakeven are a wonderful thing, indeed. It's what hedge funds strive for.

However, what if a currency's value is falling, but your bias is that it should be rising? Do you skip the trade? Perhaps, or you can plan short-term trades. Trade it down for a while and profit on the short-term and then reinvest the profits back into the currency when it rises again.

This shows you that your bias is not enough. A bias takes a long time to develop or change. However, a currency changes value every second of the day. It rises and falls constantly. As a currency trader, it's your job to take advantage of these value changes.

Some value changes are short-term, such as hours or days. Some are long-term such as weeks or months. Some are with your bias. Some are against. As a forex trader, you can profit from all these changes in currency valuations, if you plan your trades smart.

Elements of a Smart Plan:

- Market Analysis
- Fundamental Analysis
- Technical Analysis
- Risk Analysis
- Trade Analysis

CHAPTER 8

Market Analysis

B efore you go to battle, you should know your enemy. Ideally, you would also know where that enemy is going and how it plans to get there. If so, you can get there first, set up fortifications, and prepare for your enemy's arrival . . . and doom.

You can't set a trap for price if you are following and reacting to the market. You need to plan and maneuver ahead of the action.

As a reminder, according to the *Art of War*, the first thing a general must do is gather intelligence. In forex trading, the first thing you need to do is define two things:

1. Speed of the market.
2. Momentum of price.

Please note there is a difference between marketspeed and price momentum.

- Speed is *how* the market is moving.
- Momentum is *where* price is going.

SPEED OF THE MARKET

Start your market analysis with speed. How is the market moving today? Is it range bound or is it trending? Here is an important trade hint: A market will maintain its speed until something fundamentally changes market bias.

Speed is a measurement of the market. To measure speed use medium term moving averages. For instance, you can use a combination of exponential moving averages (EMAs) such as:

- 20/60
- 21/55
- 34/89

Whatever seems to work for you is fine. At FX Bootcamp, we use 21/55. They are both numbers from the Fibonacci sequence, as most of our settings are.

Based on the angle and separation between these two moving averages, you will be able to define the speed of the market:

- A steep angle and large separation will indicate a fast moving and trending market.
- A shallow angle and narrow separation will indicate a slow moving and ranging market.

Figure 8.1 is an example of a market with a good amount of speed. It is moving up fairly quickly. This is because price is above the 21 EMA. Also note that the 21/55 EMAs are moving upward and the distance between the

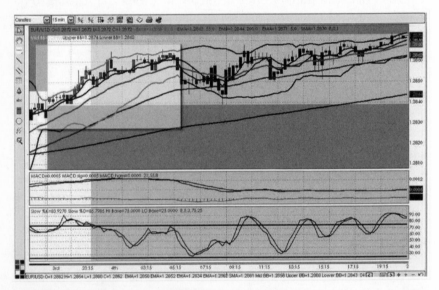

FIGURE 8.1 Market With a Good Amount of Speed
Source: DealBook® 360 screen capture printed by permission. © 2008 by Global Forex Trading, Ada MI USA

two is fairly large. Remember, steep angle and wide separation indicate a fast moving market that is trending.

Why is this knowledge important? Two reasons:

1. You can choose the right tools for the job.
2. You can adjust your risk tolerance.

The Right Stuff

- If the market is trending, Fibonacci studies and pivot point analysis work great.
- If the market is range bound, oscillators such as MACD or stochastics work well, in conjunction with Bollinger bands.

Pay attention to the behavior of the market and choose the right tools for the job. They will give you a better picture of what is actually happening. It's not enough just to have technical indicators. It's more important to know when to use them. It will keep your analysis sharp.

All lumberjacks will need an axe to cut down trees in the forest. Smart lumberjacks make sure their axes are sharp.

Appropriate Risk Tolerance

Forex traders should adjust their profit targets, or trade expectations, based on the current speed of the market.

If the market is moving quickly, it is likely to keep doing so. Do not bet against the speed of the market. Trade with the market and ride it for all it's worth: Your expectations are set fairly high.

If the speed of the market is slow, the market is more likely to consolidate and profit potential is diminished. Traders need to adjust their expectations and risk tolerance. Your expectations should be set fairly low.

Figure 8.2 shows the same market a few hours later. The market is changing. Price is still above the 55 EMA, so the market is still moving upward, it is just moving upward more slowly. The speed of the market as slowed. This is called a "step down."

Steep Stepping

The medium term moving averages act like steps on a flight of stairs. When the market is slowing down, it will "step down" from the 21 EMA to the 55 EMA. This will also reduce the steepness and the separation of the moving averages. It is not a sign of the market reversing, just a sign that the market is slowing down. Conversely, the market can "step up" from the 55 EMA to

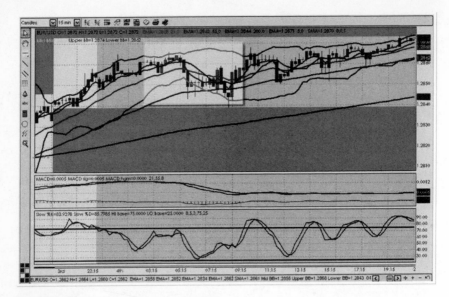

FIGURE 8.2 Market Speed Is Slowing
Source: DealBook® 360 screen capture printed by permission. © 2008 by Global
Forex Trading, Ada MI USA

the 21 EMA indicating that the market has pickup speed. In this case, you
would be able to increase your expectations and profit targets.

In Figure 8.2, some traders would have shorted this currency pair. They
may have even made a profit, but because the market is still moving upward, albeit more slowly, they are betting against the market. This is more
risky than trading with the market, and it is less likely to yield much profit.

More risk and less profit potential is *not* a conservative or ideal spot
trade. You may want to pass on the trade and wait for an opportunity to go
long when the market returns to its upward direction.

How do you know when this happens? You need to measure the momentum of price, our next topic. You will then have speed of the market
and momentum of price aligned. Although it is not a guarantee of success,
it is clearly more ideal.

Before we move onto price momentum, let's discuss a slow market.
In Figure 8.3 you will notice that price is supported by the 55 EMA. This
indicates a slow moving market.

In a slow market, you should lower your trade expectations and lower
your risk tolerance. As long as price is above the 55 EMA, the market is
moving upward, it just isn't moving upward very fast.

A trader is not likely to catch a big breakout or huge profits in a slow
moving market. In fact, the longer the market behaves this way, the more

likely the market will reverse. A reversal is confirmed when the medium term moving averages cross against each other.

When the 21 is above the 55 EMA, the market is moving up. When the 21 is below the 55 EMA, the market is moving down.

Currency markets trend well. Therefore, never assume a currency pair *will* reverse. Let the charts prove to you the currency pair *has* reversed and base your trade plans on the new direction.

In the slow market highlighted in Figure 8.3, a trader will use oscillators and Bollinger bands to trade while the market is range bound or in consolidation. A trader would continue to do this until there was either a step up in the speed of the market, or a reversal cross of the 21/55 EMAs.

Figure 8.3 shows neither. This is likely because of the time of day. Most of the highlighted area is after the professional London and New York traders have gone home at the end of the trading day.

Figure 8.4 is an excellent example of a market that picks up speed at the beginning of a new trading day and maintains it until the end of a trading day.

Isn't Forex 24 Hours a Day?

Why do I keep talking about the start and finish of trading days and trading sessions? It is true; the forex market is open 24 hours Monday through

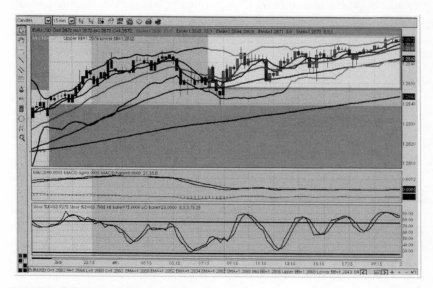

FIGURE 8.3 Slow Moving Market
Source: DealBook® 360 screen capture printed by permission. © 2008 by Global Forex Trading, Ada MI USA

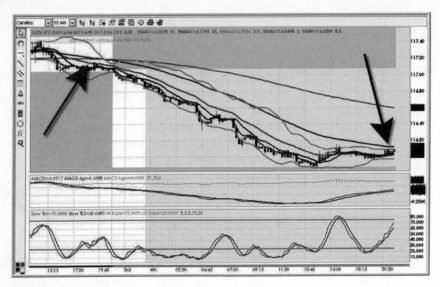

FIGURE 8.4 Market Picks Up and Maintains Speed
Source: DealBook® 360 screen capture printed by permission. © 2008 by Global
Forex Trading, Ada MI USA

Friday, but think about the human element of trading. Professional traders
work at banks or trading firms. They keep regular hours, just like any other
worker. They likely have a spouse and children. This means they go to
work, make some trades, and then go home in time for dinner with the
family.

So the market may never close, but keep an eye on the clock. Pay attention to the London open (6 to 8 A.M. London time), the New York open (6 to
8 A.M. New York time) and the London close (5 to 6 P.M. London time). The
markets move when these traders open and close their trades for the day.

According to the Bank for International Settlements' Triennial Central
Bank Survey of Foreign Exchange Activity, "The United Kingdom remains
the single largest centre of foreign exchange activity with 34.1 percent of
global turnover in April 2007." Therefore, you don't want to miss trading
during the London trading session, roughly (6 A.M. to 6 P.M.) London time.
Not only are the London boys trading, most other professional traders from
all over the world are trading at that time, as well, and it is not included in
those BIS stats. That is only activity flowing through U.K. sources.

In any case, trade with the herd. Because technical analysis is a self-
fulfilling prophecy, the odds of your success are highest during these hours.
I encourage you to not trade the other 12 hours of the day.

Figure 8.4 gives you great example of a reversal cross, an increase of speed to the downside, and a step down to the 55 EMA at the end of the day. You should have been confident in shorting this currency pair all day because of the speed of the market.

MOMENTUM OF PRICE

There are many definitions of momentum. Here are some definitions that are rolled into my own use, as observed in forex trading:

1. In quantum mechanics, momentum generally describes a physical system and corresponds to an observable phenomenon.

2. In mathematics, it is the force of movement; impetus, as of a physical object or course of events.

3. In philosophy, momentum is derived from "moment," the present time or any other particular time.

4. In geometry, momentum is the product of a physical quantity and its directed distance from an axis.

In forex trading, I define momentum as the direction of price, at the moment, in relation to the speed of the market. What is price doing at the moment?

Measuring Momentum

Momentum is a measurement of current price action; what price is down right now? Therefore, to measure momentum of price use short-term moving averages. For instance, you can use a combination of EMAs such:

- 3/5
- 5/8
- 8/13

Whatever seems to work for you is fine. At FX Bootcamp, we use 5/8. Once again, they are both numbers from the Fibonacci sequence, as most of our setting are.

Note: the 8 is a simple moving average, unlike all our other moving averages, which are exponential moving averages. I found this to be effective, as it slows the study down. As a conservative trader, I want the moving averages to cross less often, not more.

Based on the angle and separation between these two moving averages, you will be able to define the momentum of the market:

- A steep angle and large separation will indicate that momentum is increasing.
- A shallow angle and narrow separation will indicate that momentum is decreasing.

Centrifugal Momentum

Momentum is either pushing price up or it is pushing price down. If price is not moving up or down, there is no momentum. Obviously it's ideal to trade with momentum, but not all momentum is created equal. Imagine a ball attached to the end of a rope. If you swing the rope around and around in one direction, the ball naturally wants to fly outward. This is centrifugal force. This force is created from the energy of the spinning rope.

This is similar to forex trading. The market is the force spinning upward or downward. The ball is the price. The direction the price moves in depends which direction the market is moving. If the market is spinning up, then price finds it easier to rise. If the market is spinning down, price finds it easier to fall.

Water always finds the path of least resistance. Similarly, currency prices in the forex market prefer to find the path of least resistance or support. Centrifugal momentum means price naturally wants to flow in the direction of the overall market. Using your moving averages as a guide, centrifugal momentum is an alignment of price action with market action. For example, after the 21/55 has crossed down, a centrifugal trading strategy entails only shorting a currency pair each time the 5/8 crosses down as well.

With centrifugal momentum, the faster the market is moving, the farther away price wants to move. However, all markets exhaust and price gets tugged back. This force is called centripetal momentum.

Centripetal Momentum

The market is not always aligned. Does this mean you shouldn't trade? Sure you can trade. However, just be aware that you are trading against the market and assuming additional risk.

Centripetal momentum is trading against the market. It can be done successfully and profitably, but not until you are an accomplished trader. Personally, I don't think you need to trade every move. I think you should wait and trade with the market. Swim into the middle of the river and float downstream. It's just easier than trying to swim upstream against the current. Go with the flow.

Using your moving averages as a guide, centripetal momentum is 5/8 crosses in the opposite direction the 21/55 is moving. When these crosses occur, price and market are not aligned. Price has momentum, but it's moving across the grain.

In Figure 8.5, you will see the direct benefits of trading with centrifugal momentum. Trades that occurred when price momentum was aligned with the speed of the market yielded about 150 pips. Trading against the market still yielded a profit but only 75 pips.

A trader could see this as half the profit or as twice the risk. In either case, trading against the market is less ideal than aligning price *with* the market.

Inertial Momentum

My definition of inertial momentum is "the tendency of price to resist acceleration; the tendency of price to stay at rest. Inertial momentum is the resistance or disinclination to motion, action, or change of action of price." In simple terms, inertial momentum is when price is not moving up or down, but sideways: Price has no momentum.

Inertial momentum is seen by excessive crossing of the 5/8 moving averages. Too much crossing of the short-term moving averages indicates lack of direction of momentum, a slowing of the market, and a lack of trading from traders.

Figure 8.6 shows that trading with lack of momentum will surely result in a losing trade. Price isn't going anywhere at the moment. It's more ideal to wait for momentum to pick up and for the market to show some sort of direction before your pull the trigger.

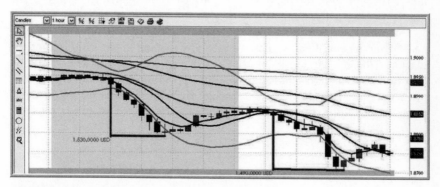

FIGURE 8.5 Trading with Centrifugal Momentum
Source: DealBook® 360 screen capture printed by permission. © 2008 by Global Forex Trading, Ada MI USA

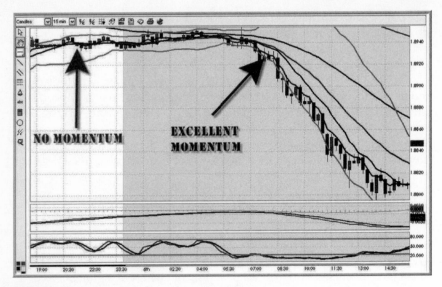

FIGURE 8.6 Trading with Lack of Momentum
Source: DealBook® 360 screen capture printed by permission. © 2008 by Global
Forex Trading, Ada MI USA

SUMMARY

So, as you can see, not all trade opportunities are the same. Some can be more profitable than others, and some are almost certainly losers. I hope the use of momentum and market will help you identify your opportunities and your threats. Sure, all trades can potentially lead to a profit or to a loss. However, generally speaking, try not to trade against the market. The market is bigger than you.

You can increase your odds of success throughout your entire trading career but especially as a novice trader, by trading in the direction of the market. This is when market and price are aligned: centrifugal momentum.

You don't need to trade every trading opportunity nor should you chase price up and down. Go with the market. Go with the flow. Enjoy the ride. It should last until something fundamentally changes . . . a shift in bias.

CHAPTER 9

Fundamental Analysis

F undamental analysis is not a study of price; it is the study of the market. It is the study of economic data, not of charts, like technical
analysis is.

Economic data will give you clues about the health of an economy and
its possible effect on the value of that economy's currency. Fundamental
analysis will not tell you when to get into or out of a trade. It will, however, help you develop an opinion on where the market is going in the
long-term.

ECONOMIC ANNOUNCEMENTS

*An object at rest tends to stay at rest and an object in motion
tends to stay in motion until acted upon by a greater force.*
—Sir Isaac Newton, First Law of Motion

What is a currency worth? What is its fair market value? That is the
fundamental question in currency trading. If a currency is appreciating in
value, you buy it. If it is depreciating in value you sell it. But how do you
know if it is likely to rise or fall in value? A study of economic data is
needed.

Luckily, economic data is collected by governments and released on a
regularly scheduled basis. As a currency trader, you are interested in finding evidence of just one thing: inflation.

Why are forex traders interested in inflation? Interest rates. In a nutshell, this is how the global currency markets work:

Increased inflation → increased interest rates → increased currency appreciation.

GLOBAL MONEY FLOW

Central banks are in charge of maintaining a stable economy for their nation. They study the economic data on an ongoing basis.

If their economies grow too quickly, prices surge and everything becomes far too expensive. To slow their economies to a reasonable pace with fairly stable prices, these banks have many tools at their disposal, the most visible of which is raising interest rates.

This makes money more expensive and slows the economy down thereby keeping prices at healthy levels.

Conversely, if the economy is growing too slowly, a central bank has the ability to lower interest rates, thereby making money cheaper and often easier to obtain. This spurs borrowing, which spurs spending, which spurs the economy and increases demand.

INTEREST RATES AND CURRENCY VALUES

Let's briefly revisit a key concept. You live in a small town. Right in the middle of it are two banks, directly across the street from each other. Both are exactly the same distance from your home, offer the exact same services and both have attentive staff.

One is willing to pay you 3.5 percent interest on your money in deposit at the bank. The other is willing to pay you 7 percent interest on money you deposit with it. Which would you prefer: more money or less?

Money flows around the globe just that way. Investment flows away from low interest countries and toward high interest countries because the higher interest yields provide better returns for the money. Central banks, hedge fund managers, corporate financial officers and forex traders all want the same thing: more profit, not less.

But remember, investment flows this way not just because interest rates are high but because the developed economies with high interest rates are likely booming, and developed economies with low interest rates are likely not doing so well.

Economies that are booming are also attracting investors to their stock markets, stuffing corporations with cash to hire their citizens, increase spending and making a hot economy even hotter. Investment spurs success. This means money and investment is flowing into that red hot economy from all corners of the world.

Take this for example:

Australia has high interest rates because its economy is doing great, largely due to China buying up all its natural resources, such as coal.

Let's say because of this, China invests money into the company that owns the Australian coal mine, so it can produce more coal for China more quickly. China can't give the Australian company Chinese yuan; it needs Australian dollars. Therefore, China must buy Aussie dollars first, then invest them into the local mining company. This creates an increase in demand for Aussie dollars. Increased demand raises the value of currency.

Also, if a Japanese investor wants to put money into an Australian bank because it pays much more interest, he cannot deposit yen. The investor must first purchase Australian dollars then deposit them in the Australian bank.

Once again, the purchase of Australian dollars had increased demand for the local currency, contributing to its appreciation, and further spurring the economy and giving Australia's central bank more reason to consider raising interest rates even higher.

You may notice that there seems to be either an upward or downward self-perpetuating cycle here. Expanding economies have increasing inflation, which pushes up interest rates, which attracts global investment, which expands the economy more, which boosts inflation more, which raises interest rates more, which attracts even more global investment, which expands the economy even more, and so on.

The opposite will happen in economies with low interest rates. Case in point: Japan. The Japanese have had low interest rates and a lackluster economy for 12 years. This is exactly why currencies trend so well.

So, if I were to adapt Newton's Laws of Motion to how the currency markets naturally behave, they would read this way: "An economy at rest tends to stay at rest and an economy in motion tends to stay in motion until market bias of the economy has fundamentally changed."

The driving forces behind currency trends are the fundamentals of their economies. Fundamental analysis is the study of economic indicators and the market bias that these reports create.

MARKET BIAS

Market bias is the majority opinion of all traders in the currency market. Everyone has equal access to the economic announcements the instant they are released. There are no secrets in forex. Information is available to everyone.

As new information is announced, the latest consumer price index (CPI) report for the United States for example, everyone in the market will have access to the results. This new information may or may not change each trader's opinion about the health of the U.S. economy. What is important is that the new data is priced into the currency immediately.

A low CPI reading may be a sign to some traders that the U.S. economy is slowing. They may ponder how the central bank, a.k.a. the Fed, will interpret this low number. Does it mean there is less inflation? Perhaps the low CPI is evidence the Fed should lower interest rates? If this is the opinion of the trader, then the trader would consider selling USD.

In today's Internet-powered world, all active forex traders would get this CPI data immediately. If the majority of currency traders are also worried about the low CPI data, then the market bias for the U.S. dollar could turn negative. In this case, you may see the U.S. dollar decline in value the second the poor CPI data hits the market and traders around the world start selling greenbacks.

Remember, market bias is the majority opinion of all traders in the market. Bias is shaped by all known information. This information primarily comprises the economic reports that are announced on a regular basis, but could also be related to geopolitical events, weather and natural disasters, and anything else traders consider important to the economies and currencies they are trading.

Currency trading is herd mentality at its best. This means that the markets don't always move on pure logic alone. Even if it's based on greed or fear and not solid economic data, market bias still will move the markets and it is directly related, even if not logically related, to this data. However, careful study of economic announcements will align you with the long-term trends of the currency market, and they should not be ignored.

ANNOUNCEMENT CALENDAR

Earthquakes, terrorism, hurricanes, or sudden political instability can throw the forex market into turmoil, but these events are fairly rare and cannot be planned for. However, the vast majority of the spikes in the forex markets are due to economic announcements that are scheduled on a regular basis. Currency traders must pay close attention to this calendar.

Why?

If the market is in motion or at rest, it will continue to be so until something fundamentally changes. The change occurs when bias is revised based on new information that hits the market and affects the majority opinion of the traders in the market. This happens when an economic report is announced.

Hence, the market may change its behavior, sometimes dramatically, based on fundamental announcements scheduled on the day's calendar. Therefore, it would not be advised to enter a trade that has been planned based on what the market has been doing just before an economic announcement is released.

What has been happening may not continue to happen after the news is released. The speed of the market and momentum of price often changes when these announcements come out. You should be keenly aware of the scheduled announcements on the calendar.

Wait for the announcement to be released to the public and see if it has changed the market bias. If it has, create a new trade plan. If not, continue as planned. This means every currency trader should review the calendar, such as shown in Figure 9.1 from FXStreet.com, before they even open their charts.

If these news events do add volatility to the market, they can provide short-term trade opportunities. Traders should be cautious when trading the news as a short-term event, as apposed to the longer term bias, because there are unique risks associated with this type of trade.

- The market can be choppy. This means price spikes up and then down and then back up again. In this case, all traders are knocked out with a loss, regardless of the direction they traded.

FIGURE 9.1 FXStreet.com Calendar

- Some news events can create slippage. This means you pull the trigger, along with tens of thousands of other traders, at the exact same time. A broker often has trouble processing the volume and may take up to 30 seconds to put your order into the market, but by then the price may have changed dozens of pips from where you thought you'd entered.
- Some brokers have variable spreads. It often saves you a pip or two when things are quiet, but at news time that can widen—sometimes dramatically. This is bad if you are trying to enter an order, as the order becomes very expensive. However, the wide spreads can kick you out of a trade you entered an hour before the news. Recently, when Canadian economic news was released on a very popular variable spread broker, the spread on the USD/CAD jumped to 60 pips!

So be careful; trading the news as an event is risky. Sometimes it proves to be quick money, but you take the risk of a quick loss as well. A conservative trader will not need to trade this way, but it's an option if you want it.

Just remember, if you had your spread widen to 15 pips and had 15-pip slippage, you'd start your trade 30 pips in the hole. I prefer conservative trades when the market is moving smoothly—it's less risky!

SUMMARY

In Chapter 9, we discussed how a trend will last until something fundamentally changes. This change in bias is created from new information from news releases, weather, or geopolitical events. But what if bias doesn't change? Then expect more of the same.

If you see a long-term trend in play, look for opportunities to trade with it. You then use technical analysis to plan entry strategies for pulling the trigger—our next chapter.

CHAPTER 10

Technical Analysis

T echnical analysis is not a study of the market; it is the study of price. Unlike fundamental analysis, it is the study of charts, not of economic conditions. Chart technicians examine their charts to look for reasons to enter and exit their trades based on past performance of price.

SELF-FULFILLING PROPHECY

What is interesting is that technical analysis does not drive the trends of currencies, but it certainly does affect price behavior with amazing accuracy.

Why does technical analysis work? The vast majority of currency traders use technical analysis, therefore technical analysis works because so many traders are behaving in predictable ways based on their use of technical analysis. There are many mathematical studies and trading techniques used in technical analysis. Some are extremely complex theories and others are really quite simple. I'm a big fan of easy.

As a frequent speaker at forex conferences around the world, I've seen a lot of technical analysis techniques outlined in presentations given by other speakers. I will never forget one particular speaker who gave an incredibly detailed seminar about his outrageously complicated technique. It was amazing! No one could figure out what he was talking about. Then, about 45 minutes into his one hour speech, he realized that he had made a mistake. After flipping through his notes and sorting through some slides, he left his audience totally confused.

Remember, because technical analysis is a self-fulfilling prophecy, it works best if everyone is behaving in the same way. Maybe the speaker actually used his technique profitably, but he may be the only one in the world trading that way.

In my humble opinion, simple is better. Using a simple technique, many traders will likely see the same patterns on their charts as you do and everyone will react to the technical analysis in predictable ways.

In simple terms, if many traders see the same thing on their charts and react in similar ways to what they see, then price will respond in accordance with their behavior. For example, if price runs into resistance on a chart and reverses, it's only reversing at resistance because many traders saw the resistance and began to reverse their position.

Hence, the price reversal was a self-fulfilling prophesy. Price reversed at resistance only because many traders thought it was reversing and reversed their position, thus, reversing price.

With this in mind, I like to keep my technical analysis simple. Complex analysis limits the number of traders who will use such an analysis, thereby limiting the effects of the analysis in the first place. The more traders who are doing similar analysis and responding to the analysis in similar ways, the better the analysis will work.

Therefore, technical analysis is a numbers game. The more traders doing the analysis and responding to the analysis, the better the analysis works. More traders are capable of doing simple technical analysis, so I think simple is best. I never try to outsmart the market. I use simple technical analysis to attempt to figure out *what the market wants to do* and join the herd.

Three simple types of technical analysis include:

1. Range
2. Trend
3. Pivots

RANGE ANALYSIS

Range is the distance between support and resistance for current *price* action. It is the space between the top and bottom of recent activity. To identify support and resistance of price and thereby its current range, you need at least three points, but in many cases, range will provide you with many more, clearly outlining support and resistance.

In an uptrend, you will need at least two points to identify resistance and at least one point to identify where support likely is. You won't know if it is support for sure until it is retested, but you can anticipate that it may be.

In a downtrend, you will need at least two points to identify support and at least one point to identify where resistance likely is. You won't know if it is resistance for sure until it is retested, but you can anticipate that it may be.

Honing on the Range

Price moves in waves. Even if the long-term trend is up or down, price will move in the direction of the trend in waves. Each wave has a peak and trough. A peak will consist of a candle or small group of candles that create a higher high. A trough will consist of a candle or small group of candles that create a lower low. See Figure 10.1.

The range is the distance between support and resistance peaks and troughs. So, while in a range, it is a good idea to identify support and resistance. To do so, it may be helpful to draw horizontal lines at points where peaks and troughs seem to be level, such as the double bottom in the preceding figure.

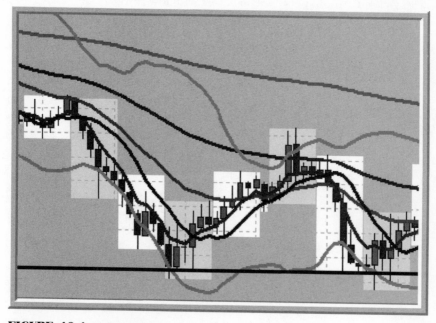

FIGURE 10.1 A Range Low
Source: FX Bootcamp, LLC (www.fxbootcamp.com)
DealBook® 360 screen capture printed by permission. © 2008 by Global Forex Trading, Ada MI USA

You need two or more level troughs to identify support in a downtrend. You need two or more level peaks to identify resistance in an uptrend. The more of either that exist in your chart analysis, the more likely other traders will also see the support or resistance and react to these levels. So remember, more is always better.

In Figure 10.2, you will notice that price touches, but does not break, support 10 times. Each time that price respects this support level, it increases the chance of price reversal to the upside.

Finally, after spending an hour at support, the bears gave up and the bulls went on a buying spree. Notice the bullish engulfing candle as price begins its ascent. Engulfing candles at support or resistance are great clues that something important is happening to short-term bias; more about that later.

Before reading any further, look closely at Figures 10.3 and 10.4. What story is speed and momentum trying to tell you? How could they be helpful to you while trading in this range? Can you spot the range?

There is only one question a trader should be asking himself at this point: Will price stay within this range or break out of the range?

If price stays within the range, you can sell at the top and buy at the bottom, however, this usually forces you to make many trades and often with very little profit per trade: high risk with low reward.

For example, let's say you are trading the Cable (GBP/USD) in a 25-pip range. If your forex broker charges you a 4-pip spread each time you trade this currency pair, then the perfect trade yields only 21 pips. However, there are no perfect traders, so don't assume you'd trade perfectly.

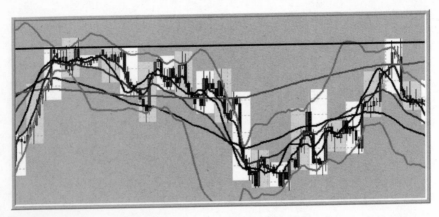

FIGURE 10.2 A Range High
Source: FX Bootcamp, LLC (www.fxbootcamp.com)
DealBook® 360 screen capture printed by permission. © 2008 by Global Forex Trading, Ada MI USA

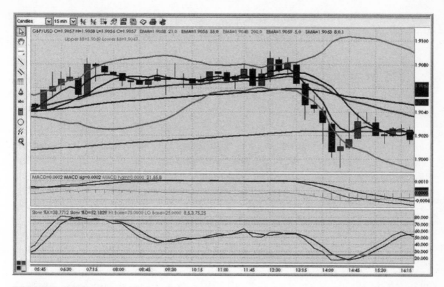

FIGURE 10.3 Blind Range Top
Source: FX Bootcamp, LLC (www.fxbootcamp.com)
DealBook® 360 screen capture printed by permission. © 2008 by Global Forex Trading, Ada MI USA

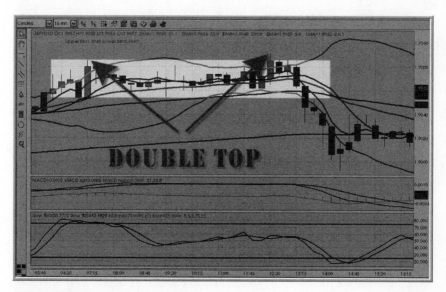

FIGURE 10.4 Range Top Revealed
Source: FX Bootcamp, LLC (www.fxbootcamp.com)
DealBook® 360 screen capture printed by permission. © 2008 by Global Forex Trading, Ada MI USA

More likely, you'd wait a little to see if price is continuing to respect the support and resistance in the range. Therefore, you're trading a little after price has already reversed direction. This means you'd be lucky to profit only 10 pips in this trade.

On top of this, you always run the risk of price breakout out of the range, thereby giving you a loss that could wipe out all the previous small winners you just made.

Let's say you placed a buy order at support in the range. However, instead of price moving back up as you expected, it breaks below support and price begins to quickly fall. You could easily lose 30 pips in a situation like this. Even if you are quick, this one bad trade could wipe out three good trades.

So how do you know if price is likely to stay within the range or break out of the range?

Speed and Momentum

This is where you really put speed of the market and momentum of price to good use in your analysis. With lots of speed and strong momentum, the range will likely be broken. With little speed and weak momentum, the range will likely hold and continue.

Once again, before reading any further, look closely at Figure 10.5. What story is speed and momentum trying to tell you? How could they be helpful to you while trading in this range?

Take a look at Figure 10.6, an example with range well defined. Note that resistance had previously been tested early in the range. However, at that time, momentum was not strong. In fact, momentum was braiding, so in this case there was actually no price momentum.

You will also notice that the speed of the market is slowing. The market is moving up, however, the angle is flattening and the separation is narrowing. This indicates that the market is slow and slowing down further. Based on speed of the market and momentum of price, with little speed and weak momentum, the range will likely hold and continue.

Now take a look at Figure 10.7. Price is testing resistance again. There is little, perhaps even no, change in speed or momentum. However, after 45 minutes (3 15-minute candles) of testing resistance, price is still in the range. The next candle is big and red and price begins to fall.

Will price fall to support and hold like it did before, or will it break? Let's take a look at the chart to see if there is any difference in speed or momentum between the two time frames.

The big difference between the two is momentum. You will notice a new momentum cross to the downside after price struggled at the double top resistance for three full candles. Failure to break is a sign of weakness.

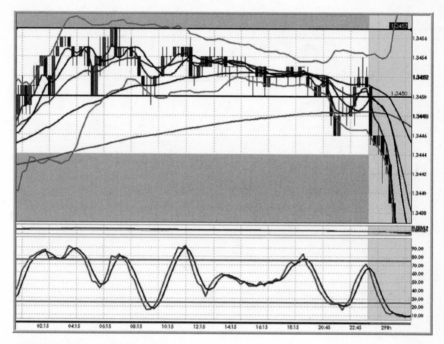

FIGURE 10.5 Range Break
Source: FX Bootcamp, LLC (www.fxbootcamp.com)
DealBook® 360 screen capture printed by permission. © 2008 by Global Forex Trading, Ada MI USA

It seems that price's inability to break resistance has attracted a lot of bears to the market, and this new selling pressure has changed price momentum to the downside and it is increasing, based on the steep angle and widening separation between the short-term moving averages, suggesting even more selling pressure.

Also, note speed as support in the range is being tested. Earlier, the speed of the market was pointing up. Now the medium term moving averages look like they are about to cross down. If this happens, this will confirm that the market and price are both falling. Ideally, a trader would only sell in this sort of circumstance.

Role Reversals

Support and resistance are fickle. They reverse roles each time they are broken. For example, if support is broken, it often becomes resistance. Conversely, if resistance is broken, it often becomes support.

Why the role reversal?

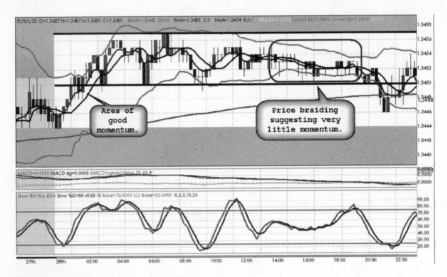

FIGURE 10.6 Range Break Clue # 1
Source: FX Bootcamp, LLC (www.fxbootcamp.com)
DealBook® 360 screen capture printed by permission. © 2008 by Global Forex Trading, Ada MI USA

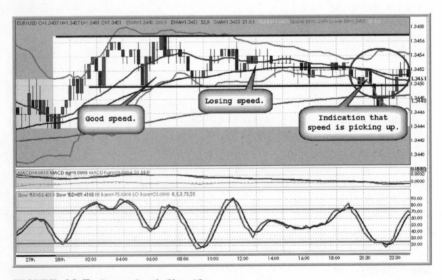

FIGURE 10.7 Range Break Clue #2
Source: FX Bootcamp, LLC (www.fxbootcamp.com)
DealBook® 360 screen capture printed by permission. © 2008 by Global Forex Trading, Ada MI USA

It's human nature; when support or resistance are broken, many traders get caught trading in the wrong direction and take a loss. When price returns to this level, these traders return to the market, this time in the correct direction. Bulls become bears or bears become bulls. That's when losing traders say, "If you can beat them, join them!" See Figure 10.8.

Second Chance

This role reversal works on two scales. One is obviously the next time a peak or trough returns to the previous level of support or resistance. The other is right after the break out.

Patient traders are often rewarded. This is often seen right after a breakout has occurred, such as in Figure 10.9.

You can see that support is clearly broken with a big red candle. Both the real body and wick have closed below the old support line. Notice the next candle. Price has returned all the way back to the support line. However, it has reversed roles: support is now resistance.

This offers all traders who missed the first opportunity to sell a second chance to do so. This is often the easier trade to make because momentum is clearly visible and support has been broken. You don't have to guess that support *will* break. A second chance trade is easy because support *has* broken; no need to guess.

FIGURE 10.8 Trader Role Reversal
Source: FX Bootcamp, LLC (www.fxbootcamp.com)
DealBook® 360 screen capture printed by permission. © 2008 by Global Forex Trading, Ada MI USA

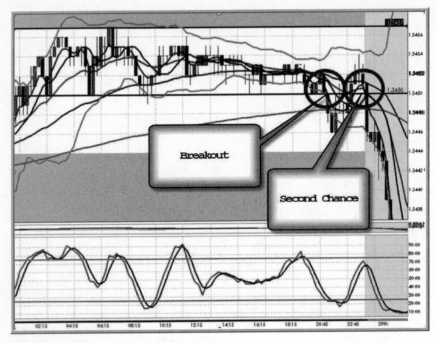

FIGURE 10.9 A Second Chance
Source: FX Bootcamp, LLC (www.fxbootcamp.com)
DealBook® 360 screen capture printed by permission. © 2008 by Global Forex Trading, Ada MI USA

Seems easy enough right? So why do so many amateur traders lose money in these situations? It's because they lack patience. Most amateur traders make two common mistakes:

1. Get into trades too late.
2. Get out of trades too early.

In this case, they missed the breakout trade because they were not planning for it. However, they see the sudden big red candle and they short right at the bottom of it. Price then returns all the way back to the old support level, and they are quickly losing pips in the retracement.

By shorting at the bottom of the breakout candle, the amateur suffers through the pullback to support and very quickly finds himself 27 pips in the hole. The amateur trader who is reacting to the market then begins to panic and exits the short trade for a loss. Oddly enough, this is when patient traders are actually entering their second chance trades.

Every trader in the world has made this mistake, so don't take it personally. Chalk it up to experience. However, planning your trades in advance and not reacting to price action will certainly help you prevent such trades. If you miss the breakout, be patient enough to wait for the pullback for your second chance.

The worst thing that can happen to a patient trader is that price action does not pull back and there is no second chance. In this case, the trader missed the trade. Oh well. It's only opportunity cost, not a real loss. Not trading is better than losing a trade. The beautiful thing about forex is that there is always another trade. Simply redo your analysis and start to plan your next trade. Don't chase price.

Advanced Technicals

Experienced traders also have other clues on this chart that suggest that price was likely to break out of the range by falling below support.

These are some of the clues:

- Bollinger bands had narrowed, suggesting that pressure was building and a breakout was coming.
- MACD had crossed to the downside.
- Stochastics had clear divergence showing weakness in the bull market at the time of the double top.

Trading Breakouts

Trading the range breakout or second chance pullback can be very profitable. When planning your breakout trade, simply measure the size of the range. Again, range is the distance between support and resistance of recent *price* action.

If the range is 72 pips, then your profit target is 72 pips from the break point. If support is broken, then your target is 72 pips below. If resistance is broken, then your first profit target is 72 pips above resistance. See Figure 10.10.

TREND ANALYSIS

Trend is like a prevailing trade wind blowing across the vast ocean. Trend is steady. As sailing a ship in the direction of the prevailing wind is easier than against, trading with the trend is also easier and often more profitable. Another way of looking at trend is like the current in a river. It's easier to swim downstream with the current than upstream against it. Go with the flow.

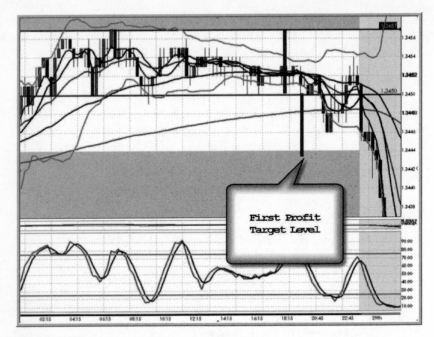

FIGURE 10.10 Set Your Breakout Target
Source: FX Bootcamp, LLC (www.fxbootcamp.com)
DealBook® 360 screen capture printed by permission. © 2008 by Global Forex Trading, Ada MI USA

Trend Spotting

Start your market analysis with speed. How is the market moving today? Is it range bound or is it trending? Here is an important trade hint: A market will maintain its speed until something fundamentally changes market bias. So if it is trending, it will likely stay trending.

To measure trend, use a long-term moving average. For instance, you can use moving averages such as:

- 100
- 200
- 233
- 800

Whatever seems to work for you is fine. The chart layout at FX Bootcamp uses the 200 EMA. Based on the angle of the 200 EMA you will be able to define the strength of the trend:

- A steep angle will indicate a powerful trend.
- A shallow angle will indicate a weak trend.

Technically Fundamental

The use of a long-term moving average, such as the 200 EMA, is a function of technical analysis. However, it helps me visualize the abstract idea of market bias.

It's impossible to know the opinion of all the traders in the market and how they are changing their opinion as new information becomes available. However, I use the long-term moving average as a visual representation of market bias.

Remember, bias is shaped by fundamental analysis or the study of all known information, primarily economic data. So to me, the 200 EMA is a technical indication of fundamental bias: trend.

True Market Value

Trend represents balance and harmony in the marketplace. The relationship between price and trend is that of a seesaw that can only move up and down. Price is either moving toward the trend line or it's moving away. Therefore, your long-term trend line can be seen as the true market value of the currency pair.

When a currency pair speeds up, it begins to move away from the long-term trend. Something has spurred the market into action. Perhaps it was something fundamental, such as an economic report recently announced to the public, or perhaps it was something technical, such as a break of resistance.

However, at some point the market will have gone too far too fast. Price will simply be out of line with its fair market value. It will have deviated too far from its trend. Price will then begin to return to the long-term moving average.

Home Sweet Home

Why does price return to the long-term trend? It does so because traders want it to return to its fair market value. Remember that the 200 EMA is the bias of the market. The bulls and the bears are always pushing and pulling on the value of a currency. The long-term moving average line is the middle ground, the market equilibrium.

The long-term trend line is where the bulls and bears, in theory, both feel relatively comfortable with the value of a currency pair: the fair market value. However, greed fuels the market, not comfort. "Fair" has nothing to do with trading!

At some point, price has just gone too far. Trader greed has pushed price to a point where fear becomes an issue. Traders with huge profits begin to fear losing their profits and begin to cash out.

Cashing out can make momentum shift direction and in turn could make the market slow from the 21 EMA to the 55 EMA as the currency pairs pull back. It will not reverse a market, but it could be the start.

A reversal will depend on what happens when price returns to the point where the profit taking first occurred. If more profit taking occurs, traders will sense the weakness and trade in the opposite direction. Momentum will shift again, the 55 will break, and price will likely return to the 200 EMA.

What happens back at the 200 EMA? That depends on the power of the trend. A powerful trend will attract traders back into the market. A majority of traders will want to trade in the direction of the prevailing trend, as it was their fundamental bias that created the trend in the first place.

A weak trend will be a sign of uncertainty of the market's fundamental bias. Perhaps their opinion of a currency is changing? If so, the trend could change, too.

Power of the Trend

Just like the other moving averages, the force of the trend can be observed by the angle of the trend line. The sharper the angle of the moving average, the more powerful the trend. In other words:

- A steep angle represents a powerful trend, and it is not likely to break.
- A flat trend line represents a diminishing trend that is more likely to break.

Remember, according to Newtonian physics, an object in motion tends to stay in motion. Therefore, if the fundamentals of a market have created a powerful trend, that trend is likely to continue until something fundamentally changes. One or two news releases are not likely to dramatically affect the trend.

Speed, Momentum, and Trend

Think of speed, momentum, and trend as a racers on a track that has a lot of twists, turns, hills, valleys, and straightaways. Just as in currency trading, this race will require skilled drivers.

At this race, there are three teams, each with a different vehicle to race with:

1. Team Speed drives a sport utility vehicle.
2. Team Momentum drives a sports car.
3. Team Trend drives a passenger bus.

Each team has advantages and disadvantages.

- **Team Speed**: The SUV can carry more passengers than the sports car, but it must turn the corners more slowly. It works best on the straight-aways and is not affected by small bumps in the road.
- **Team Momentum**: The car can take all the turns quickly and with ease, but the car often breaks down and therefore needs constant maintenance. Also, it can carry only a few people at a time.
- **Team Trend**: The bus can carry the most people at one time, but is extremely slow in the turns. It may be slow, but it is steady and offers a comfortable ride to everyone on board. It's expensive to purchase, but the cheapest to maintain. There is a lot of mass behind it. It will need time to slow down and stop if the driver wants to completely change directions.

In comparison to forex, passengers represent traders, and the turns or bumps represent volatility in price action.

I want you to paint a picture with your mind's eye. Visualize an old man easing into a hot bath.

Nice image, eh?

This is how I picture trend changing direction. It occurs very slowly and gingerly. It takes time. Trend reversals are not quick events.

Still got the naked old man image in your mind? Sorry about that. Now visualize a big passenger bus trying to do a U-turn at a narrow intersection. The bus cannot turn very quickly and, in many cases, must back up a few times to make the turn. This is a lot like how the long-term trend reverses.

The Perfect Trade

Okay, there is no perfect trade. Perfect trade setups can still yield a loss, so stop looking for a sure thing. However, some trades can be subjectively better than others.

In a perfect world, a perfect trade would be defined as one that was placed when price, market, and trend were aligned. A perfect trade would always be profitable. This is not a perfect world and there are no perfect trades that are always profitable. However, doesn't it seem logical to trade in the direction that price, market, and trend are going?

The Judge and Jury

The judge and jury are you and your trade journal. Just before you pull the trigger ask yourself, "Will I feel like an idiot if I have to document this trade in my journal as a loss? What evidence can I provide the judge and jury to support my actions? Is this a trade I can justify, even if it turns into a losing trade?"

Personally, if I trade when momentum of price, speed of the market, and the long-term trend are moving in the same direction, even if I take a loss, I don't feel like a chump entering the trade into my journal. "It's not my fault, my stupid charts lied," I tell myself.

The Three-Second Rule

If you make a winning trade, you have three seconds to cheer, jump around your office, ring a bell, high five your cat, and kiss your dog while all the angels in heaven shed tears of joy at the beautiful trade you made. Your trading greatness is a shining light in a world of darkness. You are an inspiration to all traders around the world.

When your three seconds are up, sit down, shut up, and get ready for the next trade.

If you make a losing trade, you have three seconds to pound your fist, throw your mouse, kick your chair, drop your head in shame, and cry me a river.

When your three seconds are up, sit down, shut up, and get ready for the next trade.

Winning and losing trades are both inevitable in forex. You cannot take either of them personally. You win some, you lose some. That is the way it goes. Each trade should not be that big of a deal to your overall trading career or trading account. However, if you made a stupid trade, such as chasing price or jumping in late, then you deserve the agony of entering the stupid trade into your journal. Remember it and don't do it again. Learn!

PIVOT ANALYSIS

Based on pivot points, which direction is the market likely to move? Will the market trend up or down? As mentioned, like a compass signaling direction, the key is the central pivot point.

To confirm the direction of the trend, see if today's central pivot point is above or below the previous day's pivot point. If it is above, today's price action is likely to continue upward. If it is below, it is likely to proceed downward. Just like the other technical indicators discussed in this book, a pivot trend follows the rule "an object in motion tends to stay in motion." See Figure 10.11.

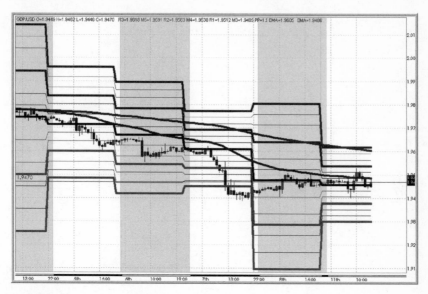

FIGURE 10.11 Pivot Trend
Source: FX Bootcamp, LLC (www.fxbootcamp.com)
DealBook® 360 screen capture printed by permission. © 2008 by Global Forex Trading, Ada MI USA

Pivot Profit Zones

With the likely direction of the day's trend now established, we need to identify likely profit targets based on our assumption of direction. At FX Bootcamp, we have two targets, one conservative, and one a little more aggressive. However, together they provide a "pivot profit zone."

For an uptrend, pivot point theory will target a profit zone of M4-R2. The bottom of uptrend trading days is M2-CPP. For downtrends, pivot point theory will target a profit zone of M1-S2. The top of downtrend trading days is M3-CPP. For the sake of simplicity: M1-M3 or M2-M4

In Figures 10.12 through 10.14, note how trend extends and then exhausts. Using nothing but the pivots, notice how this currency pair is in a clear down trend. For three days it fell from a top pivot to a likely bottom pivot profit zone. Then in the last two days, price consolidated into a pivot range, especially the last day when R1 and S1 pivot points were the exact top and bottom, as pivot point theory would suggest.

Trade Like a Cow

The "Moo Trade" is a breakout trade. It occurs when price breaks through the normal Pivot Profit Zones. This often occurs when news exaggerates the trend already in place.

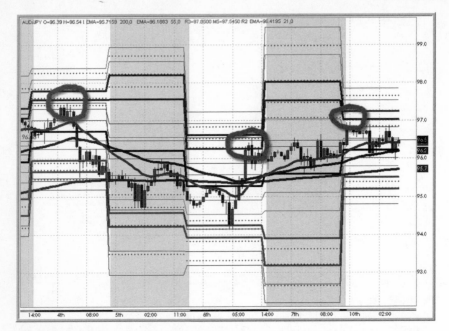

FIGURE 10.12   Pivot Profit Peak
Source: FX Bootcamp, LLC (www.fxbootcamp.com)
DealBook® 360 screen capture printed by permission. © 2008 by Global Forex Trading, Ada MI USA

"So what do you do if price breaks above R2 in an uptrend?" asked a member of FX Bootcamp, on just such a day. I responded "Keep buying until the cows come home!" Thus, the moo trade was born. See Figure 10.15.

As long as volatility remains in the market, the price action is likely to continue. Something big has moved the market—don't bet against it. Go with it. Get into the middle of the river and swim downstream with the current.

Watch the Clock

When exactly do the cows come home? At the end of the trading day, of course. For a majority of professional forex traders, that is around 5:00 P.M. London time.

Breakouts and reversals seem to happen at the opening of the London and/or U.S. session and again at the close of the London session. Why? Traders are jumping in or cashing out of trades at these times.

Remember, the forex market is essentially just a bunch of people coming together to buy and sell money. The market moves at times of the day

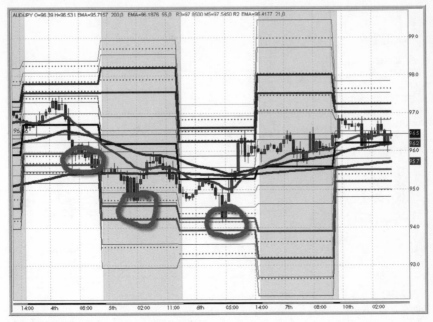

FIGURE 10.13 Pivot Profit Drops
Source: FX Bootcamp, LLC (www.fxbootcamp.com)
DealBook® 360 screen capture printed by permission. © 2008 by Global Forex Trading, Ada MI USA

when a lot of people make trades, regardless of if they are opening or closing trades. Either way, their actions at the start or finish of the trading day predictably move the market.

This is often when they have arrived at work in the morning, spent some time reviewing charts, and then make their first trade of the day. It also occurs when traders close their positions at the end of the workday, because they do not want to risk their trade overnight. When they close a long trade, it's offset by a short trade or vice versa.

In other words, jumping in and cashing out creates volatility. Watch the clock and watch the pivots! For example, if the London session is about to open or close, and price is near a pivot profit zone, be careful of reversals.

Cow Tipping

So how do you spot a "moo trade?" It's when price tips the scales and flips in the pivot profit zone.

A moo trade is a role reversal of the pivot support and resistance. It's when the M4 reversal pivot point becomes support or when the M1 reversal pivot point becomes resistance. Price usually reverses at these levels, but

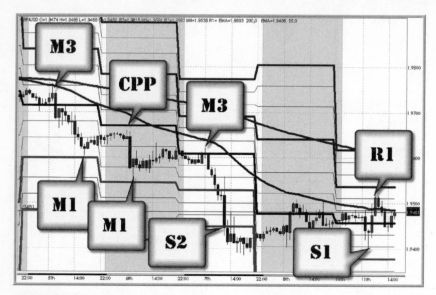

FIGURE 10.14   Pivot Profit Bottom
Source: FX Bootcamp, LLC (www.fxbootcamp.com)
DealBook® 360 screen capture printed by permission. © 2008 by Global Forex Trading, Ada MI USA

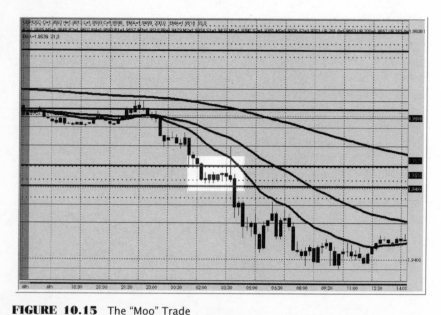

FIGURE 10.15   The "Moo" Trade
Source: FX Bootcamp, LLC (www.fxbootcamp.com)
DealBook® 360 screen capture printed by permission. © 2008 by Global Forex Trading, Ada MI USA

trend is unusually strong in this case and just keeps going; stay with the trend until it subsides.

Pivot Point Ranges

Currencies love to trend. However, not every day is a trending day. Some days, the market seems to be stalled. Unlike a moo trade that just keeps going and going, traders can also experience days when nothing seems to get going at all.

This market behavior is typical of a range trading day. As previously discussed in this book, remember to adjust your expectations accordingly and to use the proper tools for this market. In conjunction with oscillators, you can also use pivot points to assist you in trading a range bound market.

When the market seems to be moving sideways, use the primary support and resistance pivot points (S1 and R1) as a gauge of the day's likely top and bottom. When price is at these levels, look for signs of reversal, such as oscillator crossovers, momentum crossovers, and/or reversal candlestick patterns.

Also keep an eye open for role reversals, as in Figure 10.16, where onetime support becomes resistance in the future.

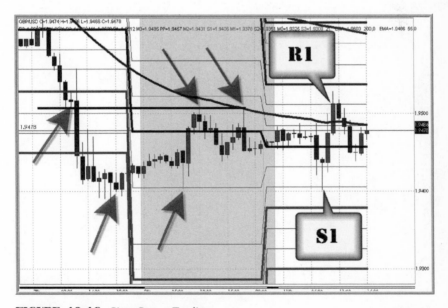

FIGURE 10.16 Pivot Range Trading
Source: FX Bootcamp, LLC (www.fxbootcamp.com)
DealBook® 360 screen capture printed by permission. © 2008 by Global Forex Trading, Ada MI USA

SUMMARY

There are endless ways and reasons to pull the trigger based on technical analysis. However, that is the easy part. Trading is fun, but forex is no game. Believe it or not, trading is not the most important aspect of being a successful forex trader.

Every time you place a trade, no matter how sound your analysis is, both technically and fundamentally, you face the real risk of losing money. It's a normal part of trading forex. Therefore, you must learn how to manage your risk.

CHAPTER 11

Risk Analysis

R isk analysis helps traders reduce greed and fear. The goal of the analysis of risk is to get into and out of trades based on what the charts say and not by how you feel. I have spoken to traders from more than 50 different countries around the world, including Australia, Japan, China, Mexico, Brazil, Canada, Mexico, England, Spain, France, Germany, Moscow, the United Arab Emirates, and, of course, from all around the United States.

The common mistake I see over and over again is that amateur traders overanalyze; trying to make up for a lack of a clear understanding of how to use their technical indicators, they wait to get as many signals as possible. They do this because of the fear of losing.

FEAR OF LOSS

This sounds like a valid strategy, but it is not. It's flawed because it's too slow. Often, the wrong indicators are used at the wrong time or for the wrong reasons. The end result is that novice traders often pull the trigger far too late.

Entering late is a stressful endeavor. The forex market moves in waves. Even if the trend is down, price will move two steps down, one step up, then three steps down, then two steps up, then down again, and so on.

A novice trader who enters late inevitably enters a short trade just seconds before price moves back up. This can put the trader at a quick loss of 20 or so pips. Then he panics and gets out just before the price returns to the downtrend. The analysis was correct; price will fall. However, the timing of the entry was poor.

The exit was emotional, based on the fear of loss. So fear of loss is present in both entries and exits. The trade was disastrous. Unfortunately, it is all too common for new traders.

You'd think professional traders would be a lot better at controlling greed and fear, right? Wrong. They just have the opposite problem. Professional traders are much more experienced at the timing of their entries. They also have a strong understanding of the underlying fundamentals. Therefore, they are better at picking the right direction and getting in.

However, professional traders are always working at letting their profits run. It's harder than you'd think. Professionals have fear of profit. It's true!

FEAR OF PROFIT

Professionals also must deal with fear, just like novice traders. Not the fear of loss, but the fear of profit. They are worried that they will lose the profit they have with their open trades. It could be a spot trade with 75 pips or a carry trade with 750 pips. The trades may still be technically valid, but out of fear, they cash out.

Some may say that you'll never go broke taking profit. However, traders have to do the hard work of analysis before making the trade. It's essential to trust the analysis and earn the pips that are deserved. Leaving pips on the table for emotional reasons is not justifiable. This is especially true for the professional traders who are managing other people's money.

Novice and professional traders alike can address their emotional fears by planning their trades in advance. This will include entries and exits based on technical analysis of the charts. By focusing on the plan and not the money, fear is reduced. If your plan was to stay in until momentum crosses, do that. Plan your trades and trade your plan. Don't worry about the money.

Every trade has two limits: one for profit and one for loss. One of these will be triggered and the trade exited. Profit or loss will come from the implementation of your logic, not by reacting to the market or being overcome by fear.

LIMITS

So you studied the speed of the market and momentum of price. You then did a quick check to see if there were any announcements that would change things. With the coast clear of any market-changing news, you identified the price range and started to create a trade plan based on a break or bounce at support and resistance, ideally in the direction of the long-term trend. You even used pivots to overlap the likely range of the market with the range of price for the identification of entries or exits. You are now ready to pull the trigger, right?

Wrong!

At this point, you may have successfully planned a trade, but we need to do a risk analysis and manage the trade.

Every trade has two limits. One is for potential profit. The other is for potential loss. Which is more important? Greed or fear?

FX BOOTCAMPER CREDO

To answer this, we can consult the FX Bootcamper credo:

1. Capital Preservation—survive at all costs.
2. Capital Acquisition—achieve the mission.
3. Capital Appreciation—win the war.

Capital Preservation

Live to trade another day. The first priority of a conservative trader is to protect his money and not do anything that may draw down his capital.

As a currency trader, you are in the business of buying and selling money. Cash is your product and your service. If you run out of money, you are out of the currency trading business. Protect your money at all costs.

Capital Acquisition

Lock in your minimal acceptable performance (MAP) for each of your trades. MAP is *not* a goal or a target. It is a minimum requirement for each of your trades. If MAP is not likely, then don't do the trade.

My personal MAP is 15 pips. To make this achievable, I seek trade setups that are likely to yield 30 to 45 pips. This means that even if my entry is not perfect, I'm still likely to be able to lock in MAP. I do this by moving my stop loss to protect my profit.

Capital Appreciation

With MAP now locked in, it's time to get aggressive. Get as many pips as you can. This is extremely important. The extra pips above MAP will pay for your losing trades, or for days you didn't trade at all. Your stop loss is protecting profit, so the worst-case scenario is walking away with only 15 pips.

At the very least, stay in your trade until momentum changes, or you reach a reversal pivot point, or hit the average daily range for the currency pair you are trading. The point is to not worry so much about the trade.

Enjoy it. It was a good trade. Let it run. The hard work is over. In this case, with a little bit of luck, advanced traders often let these spot trades turn into swing or carry trades.

LIMITS FOR LOSS

Get used to losing in forex. It's a normal part of trading. In fact, you should take pride in your losses. Do not fear them. Respect them.

When you recognize a losing trade, get out!

- Do not wait for price to come back.
- Do not ride out the storm.
- Do not double down.
- Do not be the tough guy.
- Be the wimp and cash out.
- The sooner the better.

Take Pride in Your Losses

Some of my best trading decisions were to get out of losing trades moments before the trade would have turned really ugly. A negative 28-pip trade could have been a negative 48-pip trade if I hadn't had a trade plan.

Emotional duress and mental certainty would have doomed me. When a plan has failed, it's best to abort the trade. The great thing about forex is that there are endless amounts of trades. If you are on the wrong side of a move, preserve your capital by cutting your losses and get in on the next trade.

The more emotional baggage you place on your losing trades, the worse they'll get. New traders are often ashamed of losing trades. Be ashamed of stupid trades not losing trades. You can develop your knowledge of the forex market and improve your trading skills so your stupid trades will fade into rarity. However, small losses are normal.

Remove the pride and fear from your trading. Get out when your charts tell you something has changed. Then create a new trade plan. Don't exit your trade because of emotion. Exit the trade because the charts told you to or your limit for loss has been triggered.

Momentum and Speed Change

We all love to trade. However, trades often don't turn out the way we expect. Over time, things change. You may need to adjust your strategy.

There are many strategies and indicators to use for stop losses. Let's discuss two of my favorite stops that anyone can use because they are so easy:

1. Momentum change: Exit your trade when the 5/8 crosses against you. This is a quick exit for short-term trades. Why stay with a trade if it has lost price momentum? In this situation, you risk that the pullback could turn into a full reversal. Why take that risk? Cash out and perhaps you can reenter a new trade later. Take the money and run. It's okay—the charts told you so.

2. Speed change: Exit your trade when the 21/55 crosses against you. This happens less frequently and is therefore more appropriate for medium-term swing trades.

Both momentum and speed changes are excellent opportunities for getting out as your trade becomes less ideal. They are technical indications that something has changed, and they give you permission to get out. Luckily, they help you cut your losses fairly quickly and they are easy to spot.

What? No Stop Loss?

I always use a stop loss. However, it is not there to take me out of a losing trade. It is there to protect me from catastrophic failure, such as an earthquake that knocks out all the power and cell phone towers for a hundred miles leaving my open trades at risk.

I place my stop loss order 50 pips away. It doesn't mean I take 50-pip loses. It means that if something goes terribly wrong, the worst thing that can possibly happen is that I lose 50 pips. Not the end of the world. However, in all other cases, I get out of my trades because my charts tell me to.

For example, if I went long and then momentum suddenly crosses down, I would be in a losing trade and would exit at the 5/8 cross. However, I would not likely lose very many pips, perhaps about 20 or so, depending on the currency pair. I would exit the trade because of the reversal of momentum against the trade, not my stop loss.

However, I want to emphasize that I exit because of what my charts are telling me not because my 50-pips stop was triggered or because of fear of a 20-pip loss.

Plan for the Worst

Because my stop is placed 50 pips away, I calculate my risk based on the worst-case scenario—my stop loss being triggered. It can and does happen, so I assume the loss of 50 pips. Therefore, when I am calculating how many lots I can afford to place on any particular trade, it's always based on my stop being 50 pips away, even though I have no intention of waiting that long to exit a losing trade.

The benefits of this strategy are:

- Quick and easy. I often place multiple trades on multiple currency pairs at the same time. I always base my calculations on that static 50-pip stop loss. I don't have to add or subtract my entry from the stop to figure out how many pips I have at risk. To me, it's always the same 50 pips at risk.
- Reduces leverage. Even though I plan on a 50-pip stop loss, I have no intention of letting it be triggered. Losing trades are usually revealed by the charts within 15 to 30 pips. Planning for a larger loss reduces my risk. This is because I can't afford to trade as many lots risking 50 pips as I could if I was only risking 25. In fact, it would be half as many. By reducing my lot size by half, I'm effectively reducing my risk by half. Remember, capital preservation is my No. 1 goal. Therefore, reducing my risk helps preserve my capital.

LIMITS FOR PROFIT

To me, exiting a trade for profit is basically the same as exiting for loss. I strive to simply do what my charts tell me to. As soon as things change for my trade, I look for opportunities to profit.

1. Momentum changes: Exit your trade when the 5/8 crosses against you. This is a quick exit for short-term trades.
2. Speed changes: Exit your trade when the 21/55 crosses again you. This happens less frequently and is therefore more appropriate for medium-term trades.

The benefit from either strategy is that you are *not* in the driver's seat. You simply stay in your profitable trade until the moving averages cross against you. They are a little slow and you will always leave a few pips on the table. You'll never get out at the exact top or bottom. But you will certainly catch the bulk of the move.

If in fact, you often stay in the trade a little longer than you may have planned on, you may have left a few pips on the table, but you probably still made more than if you reacted emotionally.

MORE TACTICS FOR TRADE ENTRY AND EXITS

The following is a list of additional methods and indicators that will help you decide when to enter and exit a trade:

True Limit Orders: There are times when you should take matters into your own hands. This is when you are trying to play the odds. Remember that forex is a form of fractal geometry. Simply said, there are a lot of repeatable patterns. Using limit orders is a way to try to take profit at the top or bottom of a market based on the patterns that you see repeat often.

Key Reversal Pivots: There are certain pivot points that are usually reversal points for the day's trading range, such as R2 or S2. When spot or day trading, *I always take profit at these levels.* Sometimes price blows right through these pivots and never looks back, but I'm playing the numbers, it's not very common. More often than not, I exit at or near the end of the move.

Fibots: The term "Fibot" is unique to FX Bootcamp. These are key reversal areas that are identified by Fibonacci levels overlapping with pivot points.

Fibs + Pivots = Fibots

The convergence of these two levels can often be ideal places to take profit. The support or resistance at these levels can be powerful because many traders, often using different strategies, see this reversal area, too. The more traders who see and react to the technical analysis, the more reliable the analysis is.

In Figure 11.1, you see a 121.4 percent Fibonacci extension overlapping a major reversal pivot point (M4). I will consider placing a limit order for profit at this level. Price will very often respect the Fibot and pull back. If price doesn't reverse and continues, I can always plan a reentry.

Alarms: Alarms can be literal or they can be figurative. Some trading platforms allow you to set alarms on your charts. My GFT Dealbook360, for example, is set up to text page my cell phone when an alarm is triggered. However, your alarms can also be virtual.

FIGURE 11.1   Fibonacci Extension Overlapping a Major Reversal Pivot Point (Fibot)
Source: FX Bootcamp, LLC (www.fxbootcamp.com)
DealBook® 360 screen capture printed by permission. © 2008 by Global Forex Trading, Ada MI USA

YOUR MIND'S EYE

I often talk about "painting a picture with your mind's eye." I want you to create a mental picture of what your charts will look like in the next 8, 13, 21 or so candles. You should be able to envision what your trade will look like before you get there.

Does this mean you need a magic crystal ball? Not at all! I just want you to think about your trade *before* you pull the trigger. By planning your trades in advance, and not reacting to the market, you can anticipate market action.

For example, if price is falling, but the speed of the market is still rising, do you need to short? Perhaps not; it may be prudent to wait for price to shift its momentum upward again and go long when momentum and market are aligned.

You would create this scenario in your mind. If you are looking for reasons to go long, but price is falling, where will price be likely to rise again? Back at the 21 EMA because there is still a good angle and separation between the 21/55 to the upside? Let it fall to that point and see what it does when price gets to the 21.

What will a "bounce on the 21" look like? A clear touch and two or three green candles? How about a 5/8 cross to the upside? How about a new higher high, a bullish engulfing candle or reversal pattern?

It could be any or all of these things. What is important is that you think about it first. Wait for it to happen, and if you see evidence of what you are looking for, it's your personal alarm to pull the trigger.

You've anticipated price's reaction to the speed of the market correctly. You thought about it logically and created a plan around evidence seen on the chart. It wasn't guesswork or luck. It just made sense to you. Something must be right. Get in!

DO NOTHING

Planning your trades has an immediate effect on your trading: Most of the stupid trades vanish. They fade out of your trading. You many miss a lot of trades in the beginning, as your trade planning skills are not yet fully developed. However, missing a trade is a lot better that taking losses.

Trade plans are like setting traps a few candles in front of price. Forex is all about setting traps.

Pip Trapper

Returning to the strategies in the *Art of War*, you learn that it's not ideal to attack a fortification or to corner your enemy. Even if you are eventually victorious, the victory is likely to come at a high cost. Not all victories are honorable. In trading, you can make bad trades and still make money. In the long run, your luck may run out.

As a trade strategist, you should focus on setting a trap for price. To take full control of your trading:

- Make price come to you.
- Take the high ground.
- Build your fortifications.
- Wait for the enemy to approach you.
- Attack.
- Retreat as soon as you lose your advantage, regardless if it's for victory or defeat.

If you meet your enemy on a level playing field, walk away and live to fight another day when you have the upper had. No one said war was fair.

Forex Profiteer

Repeat after me:

"I am not a forex trader."
"Only brokers make money from trading."
"I am a forex profiteer."
"I make money by profiting."

Do not start the day by opening your charts and looking for a trade. Do your technical analysis and start planning profit opportunities. Check the calendar to make sure something won't change the way the market is currently behaving. Become a profiteer. Take advantage of the predictability, or repeatability, of the market patterns. If your plans come to life, you are likely to profit. That is what you are looking for.

A level playing field in forex is a market that could go either way. It's a 50/50 chance either way. If you find that your analysis points to "maybe up or maybe down," step aside and wait for price to dictate direction for you and then trade in that direction.

Don't guess. Don't trade. Wait.

Trading Discipline

Don't trade. Sounds easy, eh? It's not. Novice traders love to trade. They often trade way too much. It's very easy to trade. Just pull the trigger. However, it's difficult to not trade. Don't focus on trading. Focus your time and energy on planning.

If you find that direction is not clear, let price choose for you and then create a plan around that. That means you must have the discipline and guts to not trade while you wait for the fog to lift.

You wouldn't fly a plane in zero visibility. You wouldn't scuba dive in zero visibility. Why trade when profitability is zero then? Wait for the fog to lift and then start planning your profit opportunities.

Remember not to chase price. If you see a big green or red candle that you did not anticipate, don't trade. Create a plan around that move. Wait for it to retrace and perhaps give you a second chance. If not, don't trade. Maybe you can catch a similar, but delayed, move on another pair based on currency correlation. If not, don't trade.

DO YOU HAVE THE GUTS?

Look into the mirror and ask yourself, "Do I have the guts not to trade?" Having control over your emotions and the discipline to not chase price is the real-world test of your long-term potential.

Remember, the number one goal of a conservative trader is to preserve capital and to not put yourself into situations where you may lose. Reacting to the market clearly puts you into a position that you are not in control of. Why did you not anticipate this move in advance? Because you did not anticipate the move, trading it is risky because you simply do not have a clear understanding of why it's moving. It could change direction any second. Step aside.

In such a situation, if you end up making a winning trade, you do not deserve the pips. You got lucky and eventually your luck will run out.

You earn your pips in your planning. If your planning didn't foresee this move, then create a new plan. Don't trade without preplanning, because you clearly missed something in your analysis and you will have no control over your destiny. Avoid the temptation of short-term gains and focus on developing long-term trading skills with patience and discipline to plan.

Unanticipated moves can happen a lot, as you can't know everything—and everything matters in forex. It's an efficient market, which means all known information is priced in immediately. News, data, weather, politics, terrorism, commodities, equities, bonds—everything matters. You can't know everything.

So, if you did not have a mental alarm painted with your mind's eye, do nothing. Preserve your capital for a situation you did anticipate. You are simply looking for opportunities to profit from situations you can anticipate in advance by planning strategies based on your technical and fundamental analysis.

Why throw all that away and trade when you have no idea what's going on?

SECOND CHANCES IN FOREX

The wonderful thing about forex is that there is always another trade. You don't have to catch all of them, and you don't need to capture every pip in each of them. You should focus on catching the bulk of the logical trades, what I call "repeatable" trades. Since these kinds of trades occur over and over, they can be planned for in advance. Soon you will become a confident trader, as you will recognize the trade setups and how to trade them. This is an inevitable result of planning your trades.

Technical analysis of charts is a form of fractal geometry or pattern recognition. In the beginning, you will find that some patterns are easier to find than others.

For example, most new traders can see head and shoulders patterns without too much trouble, but many cannot see upside down head and shoulders reversal patterns for downtrending markets. You would think they would be just as easy to spot, but inevitably they are not. However, over time, they will get easier to see, easier to plan for and eventually, easier to trade.

With this in mind, as you gain experience strategically and tactically planning your trades in advance, you will find that your successful plans are very similar to each other. Naturally, you are better at seeing some patterns than others and therefore your anticipation of the results of these patterns proves successful in your planning. As you gain experience, you will slowly add other patterns to your trading repertoire.

If you create a plan and you incorrectly anticipated price reaction, do nothing. Don't trade. Just consider creating a new plan. For example, if you were waiting for price to return and bounce at the 21 EMA, but it didn't bounce when it got there, do nothing. Something is wrong. Start a new plan.

Again, the instant gratification to trading situations that you can anticipate based on logically planning your profit opportunities in advance include the following:

- You will stop making stupid trades.
- You have more control of your trades.
- You develop constancy in your trading.
- You become a confident trader.
- Your experience makes you a better trader.

To be able to successfully trade forex day in and day out, month after month, year after year, you cannot rely on your gut instinct or your luck.

When I began to trade a forex demo account many years ago, I found I had no instinct for the market, and I had the worst luck. Zero instinct and zero luck. Every time I shorted, I would suddenly see green. It was uncanny. The more obvious the trade looked, the less it seemed to work for me. It even seemed like the market was out to get me. Price always seemed to reverse when I entered a trade just far enough to hit my stop loss—often to the pip. Was there someone out to get me? Why would someone care about me so much? What did I do to piss them off?

It's funny how attitude can change things. I can now see that the market actually tries to help me. It usually comes back and gives me a second chance. This is exactly where I used to lose money. Now it's where I make money. I owe it all to planning my trades and trading my plans. Usually, if I'm right, I profit. If I'm wrong, I didn't trade anyways, so who cares!

In my humble opinion, a successful forex trader always takes the time to develop a smart plan, as shown in Figure 11.2.

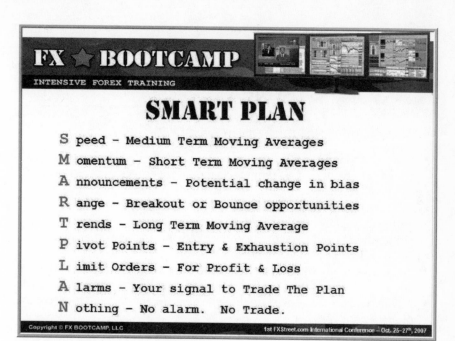

FIGURE 11.2 Sample SMART PLAN
Source: FX Bootcamp, LLC (www.fxbootcamp.com)

SUMMARY

Trade planning should put you in higher percentage trades and keep you out of bad trades. The key is to plan the trade in advance so you can implement your technical and fundamental analysis.

Sun Tzu said in the *Art of War*:

"Planning is a great matter to a general [trader];
it is the ground of death and of life;
it is the way of survival and of destruction,
and must be examined.... Before doing battle,
one calculates and will win, because many calculations
were made."

Planning your strategy so you can implement your cold, hard, logical analysis will help you manage your emotions. Management of your emotions, in turn, removes a lot of the stress of trading. Perhaps, because you have a clear head and solid analysis, your trading has a better chance of surviving and thriving.

With a strategy in place, now you need to turn your focus to your tactical implementation of your strategy.

PART THREE: SUMMARY

To recap, following are the key takeaways for Part Three:

- Speed is the study of the market.
- Speed is indicated by medium-term moving averages such as the 20/60, 21/55, or 34/89.
- Steep angle and wide separation indicate a fast-moving market.
- Momentum is the study of price.
- Momentum is indicated by short-term moving averages such as the 3/4, 5/8, or 8/13.
- Steep angle and wide separation indicate strong momentum of price action.
- Align your risk tolerance with the speed of the market and momentum of price.
- The trades that are most likely to yield a successful trade are trades that have speed and momentum aligned.
- A market at rest tends to stay at rest; a market in motion tends to stay in motion until bias has fundamentally changed.
- Bias is the majority opinion of all traders that are trading in the market.
- Opinion is shaped and reshaped constantly by all known information.
- This can be anything that directly or indirectly affects global money flow.
- The most common is economic data reports that are announced on a regular schedule.
- Such announcements can instantly change the value of a currency.
- Because economic reports are released around the world every trading day, traders should be aware when these announcements are scheduled to be released.
- Range is support and resistance of price.
- Start by identifying support and resistance. This will be the range you are trading in at the moment.
- Match your trading with the speed of the market and momentum of price.
- The faster the speed and the stronger the momentum, the more likely that support or resistance will likely be broken.
- Trends are long-term and don't change often.
- Trends represent the long-term bias of the market, as shaped by fundamental analysis.

- The trend line represents the fair market value of a currency pair.
- Price is either moving toward trend or away.
- Ideal trades are when price, market, and trend forces are moving in the same direction.
- Pivot points are a leading indicator; they help you anticipate future price action.
- Pivots outline the support and resistance areas for the market.
- Pivot points are a self-fulfilling prophecy, they only work because traders use them.
- Pivot point theory predicts an uptrend range from an M2-CPP low to a high of M4-R2.
- Pivot point theory predicts a downtrend range from a high of M3-CPP to a low of M1-S2.
- Occasionally, trends are stronger than usual and trade beyond their anticipated pivot point ranges. This is a moo trade. Stay with the trend until the momentum subsides, often at the end of the trading day.
- Range bound markets often bounce between the primary support (S1) and resistance (R1) pivot points.
- Risk analysis helps traders reduce greed and fear.
- Novice traders often trade late and exit early.
- Managing risk is about planning limits.
- Every trade has two limits: one for profit and one for loss.
- Losing trades are normal and should not be emotional.
- Spot trading exit when momentum or speeds shift against you.
- This strategy lets your profits run.
- Every trade must have a stop loss to protect against catastrophic failure.
- The stop loss is used in calculating your trading budget and managing risk.
- True profit limit orders work best with leading indicators, such as Fibonacci extensions and pivot points.
- Alarms are your signal to pull the trigger and execute your trade plan.
- Visualize your trade plan before it happens.
- If you cannot anticipate or visualize the trade in advance, do not trade.
- If you can do this, you are no longer a "trader" but a "forex profiteer."

PART FOUR

Tactical Planning

*How to Engage the Market, Pull the
Trigger, and Hit your Targets*

I n the following chapters, you will learn how to read the subtle clues
your chart may be giving you. Is the market maintaining its confidence
or are some of the traders jumping ship? This is important, because it
may be a bull market, but are there as many bulls as there used to be?
Candlesticks and oscillators can be good sources of market intelligence.

Then there are the times when trend, speed, or momentum are mean-
ingless. The market is moving on emotion more than intellect. This only occurs after important news events, which happen virtually every day. This
type of trade needs its own short-term methodology if you are going to
survive. I'll take you through it step by step.

In Part Four, you will learn:

- How to read individual candlesticks.
- How to interpret candlestick patterns.
- How to stay in your winning trades.
- How to mix trend, oscillators, and candles.
- How price action naturally cycles.
- How to trade within a range.
- How to spot trend exhaustion.
- How to see signs of reversals.
- Where to expect trend reversals.
- When to expect trend reversals.

- How to recognize trend extensions.
- How to set up for a news trade.
- How to adjust news trade risk tolerance.
- How to trade news pullbacks.
- How to trade news breakouts.

CHAPTER 12

Candlestick Patterns

There have been many books written about candlestick patterns; several feature hundreds of patterns. Don't get bogged down in trying to memorize the countless combinations that are featured in these books.

Just get to know the basic patterns, and get really good at spotting them. Other than that, don't read too much into candlestick patterns. Just a handful of patterns cover 99 percent of what happens in the real world.

A candlestick chart shows each candle as a color-coded rectangle (called the candle body) representing the range of trading between the open price and closing price of the period.

If the closing price is higher than the opening price, the candle is colored with the user specified up color, otherwise, the down color. At FX Bootcamp, green is up and red is down. Vertical lines, called wicks, are drawn protruding from the upper and lower edge of the candle body to represent the high and low extremes of trading during that period. See Figure 12.1.

In Figure 12.1, the first candle would be red. There are no wicks, just a body. This would indicate that price opened high and fell during the entire period of the candle. The second candle has no body, only wicks. This would indicate price opened, moved up and down a bit, and then closed at the same price as it opened. The last candle would be green. It has a body and wicks. This would indicate that price opened, fell slightly, then rose to close just below its highest point.

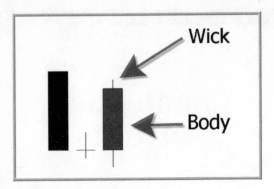

FIGURE 12.1 Candlesticks
Source: FX Bootcamp, LLC (www.fxbootcamp.com)

REVERSAL PATTERNS

The following patterns are the most common, and powerful, indicators of a candlestick reversal:

- Doji.
- Spinning tops.
- Evening and morning stars.
- Triple or double tops.
- Crown or head and shoulders patterns.

Doji

Dojis are powerful reversal indicating candlesticks and are formed when the currency price opens and closes at the same level, implying indecision in the currency's price. Dojis become a most significant reversal signal when seen after an extended rally of long-bodied candles.

Remember, a doji can only be a reversal pattern if there is a large move in place. If not, what exactly is it reversing then? If they are in a range bound market, they are much less important. Don't read too much into them without big moves behind them. See Figure 12.2.

Spinning Tops

Spinning tops denote situations where the market is having difficulty coming to a consensus on a currency's value. They portray a market in which uncertainty and indecision prevail. Neither the buyers nor the sellers have

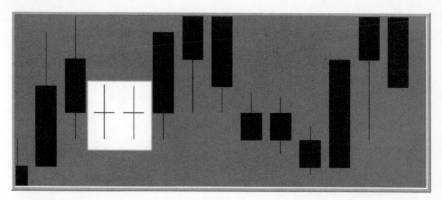

FIGURE 12.2 Doji
Source: FX Bootcamp, LLC (www.fxbootcamp.com)

a clear sense of which direction the market will head. The forces of supply and demand are equally balanced.

Like Doji, they are particularly important at the end of a long run. A spinning top is a clear sign that the powerful trend is running out of steam. See Figure 12.3.

As the old cliché goes: "When in doubt, stay out." The spinning top candles express doubt and confusion on the part of the market. Until the situation is clear, forex traders should focus on looking for confirmation of a trend reversal:

- What do your indicators say? Is there MACD divergence? Is RSI overbought or oversold?

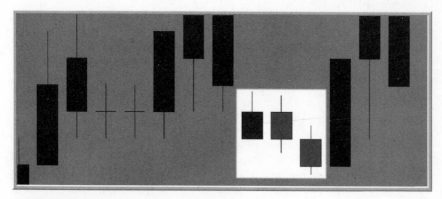

FIGURE 12.3 Spinning Tops
Source: FX Bootcamp, LLC (www.fxbootcamp.com)

- What is the next candle? Is it going against the trend after the spinning top? Did it engulf the candle before the spinning top? If so, we can see a morning or evening star.
- How far is the price reversal from the nearest exponential moving average or reversal pivot point?

The bottom line: Do not place a trade just because you see a spinning top. Use it like a trend reversal warning. It's only a heads up.

If you are in a positive trade, especially with two or three long candles going in your direction, and then you see a spinning top, you should either:

- Cash out.
- Move your stop loss closer to protect the profit or MAP.

It's a good idea to move your stop loss and let your profits run, but money in the bank is also a good idea. What should you do? Follow your trading plan.

Premature Exiting

A word of advice: If you seem to move your stops only to have price come back to knock you out and continue back in the direction you traded, don't grow frustrated. Focus on what made you move your stop prematurely in the first place. What spooked you?

Until you can manage your stops correctly, you need to practice. However, you also need to earn pips. So until you improve, you need to change your behavior. For a few trades, instead of moving your stop, just close the trade and take the profit. Even though you exited the trade, pretend that you only moved your stop and see what happens.

Many traders find that they move their stop at 15 or 20 pips profit and get stopped out at breakeven over and over. The advantage of this tactic is that you still get practice moving stops, but you also get to keep the pips. Hey, two or three trades like this add up to good pips and you are learning, too!

Why Do Spinning Tops Form?

Spinning tops form for one of two reasons:

1. The strong trend has just knocked out a lot of stop losses for people trading in the opposite direction. If this is the case, there is a good chance that they will reverse their position and put in a new order going in the direction of the new trend. This would produce a pause in the

market, seen as a spinning top. You may also see a short retracement to the 61.8 percent Fibonacci. See Figure 12.4.

2. The strong trend was likely too fast, probably producing long candles. This was good for some but likely surprised most. The lucky traders with floating profits start to feel like the good times may not last. A spinning top could be a sign of traders cashing out at the end of a trend.

Evening and Morning Stars

The star pattern occurs during a sustained trend. On the first candle we see a long body. Everything looks normal and the trend appears to have full control of price. On the second candle, however, a star candle occurs. The star can be either green or red. A star candle has a small real body and often contains a large wick.

The star communicates that the bulls and bears are involved in a tug of war, yet neither side is winning. After a sustained uptrend, those who want to take profits have come into balance with those eager to buy the currency.

A large upper shadow indicates that the trend could not sustain its probe into new ground. A potential reversal has been signaled.

In the third period, a candle with a red body emerges. This candle retreats substantially into the body of the first candle. The pattern is made

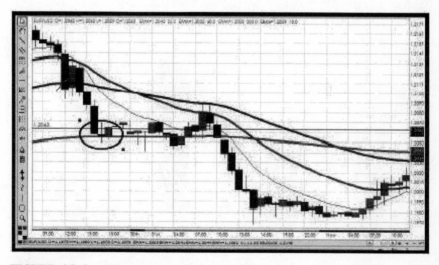

FIGURE 12.4 Spinning Top Pause
Source: FX Bootcamp, LLC (http://www.fxbootcamp.com)
DealBook® 360 screen capture printed by permission. © 2008 by Global Forex Trading, Ada MI USA

more powerful if there is a gap between the second and third period candles. The further this third candle retreats into the real body of the first candle, the more powerful the reversal signal.

Evening Star, Morning Star

The morning star formation is the exact opposite. It occurs in a downtrend and starts with a large red candle. On the second candle, a star forms. The third candle completes the reversal by closing well into the body of the first candle. See Figure 12.5.

Note that this reversal pattern is simply an established trend with an unusually big candle at the end, followed by a spinning top that is a sign of uncertainty, and then completed with a fairly large pull back candle in the opposite direction of the trend. This pattern is often seen when traders are taking profit, usually at support or resistance. Therefore, it's a great opportunity for a reversal of trend; a changing of the guard between the bulls and bears. Again, no trend, no reversal.

Triple or Double Tops

Double and triple tops are very common and very powerful candle formations. You see them on your charts because a level of support/resistance was hit by a trend. Price then retreated, gathered new strength, and attempted to pierce the support/resistance level again. See Figure 12.6.

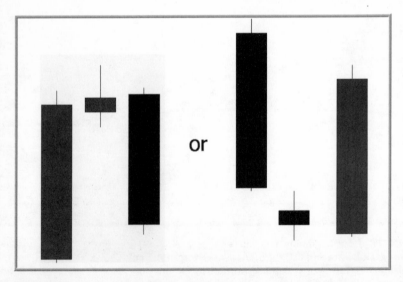

FIGURE 12.5 Evening and Morning Stars
Source: FX Bootcamp, LLC (www.fxbootcamp.com)

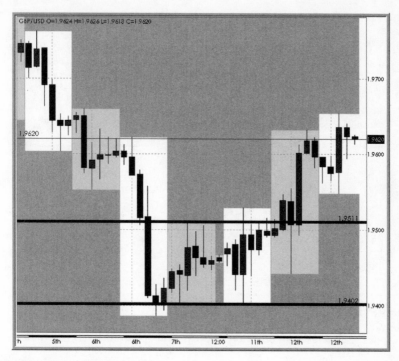

FIGURE 12.6 Double Top
Source: FX Bootcamp, LLC (www.fxbootcamp.com)
DealBook® 360 screen capture printed by permission. © 2008 by Global Forex Trading, Ada MI USA

Wouldn't you know it, price failed yet again. This is a huge signal that a reversal is likely, as the trend has just run out of steam.

While in the range produced by a triple top, pay close attention to your oscillators such as MACD or stochastic. You can do some short-term trades, then when the range is broken, you can return to spot trades after price has reversed and a new momentum appears.

Crown or Head and Shoulders Patterns

I really like crown patterns. They work the same as a triple top candle formation, with one distinct difference, the center point, or head, is higher than the other two points or shoulders. I find them easier to spot because it really is a failed continuation pattern, thereby, a "reversal pattern."

Crowns are easy to spot because the right shoulder does not make a higher high (or lower low if it is a downtrend). The top of the first shoulder becomes the new resistance level. So when you see price reverse at this new resistance level, sit up and take notice. See Figure 12.7.

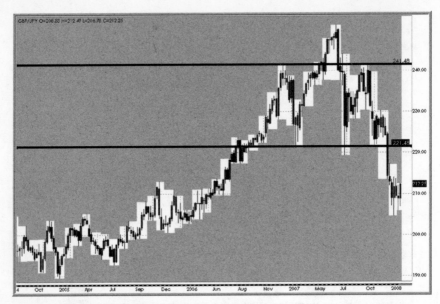

FIGURE 12.7   Head and Shoulders Pattern
Source: FX Bootcamp, LLC (www.fxbootcamp.com)
DealBook® 360 screen capture printed by permission. © 2008 by Global Forex Trading, Ada MI USA

When it breaks through the old support level created from the first shoulder's low, you will have a new trend. Support has become resistance and the trend has reversed.

Don't get bogged down in the details, however. An uptrend, for example, is a series of higher highs and higher lows. A crown pattern is simply showing you that a lower high has been made and the uptrend is likely to have reversed. That's all it is. Not too complicated when you think of it that way.

Again, if there is no previous trend in place, it's not likely a reversal pattern because there is nothing to reverse. Don't just trade the patterns, step back and see the bigger picture.

REVERSE AND CONTINUATION PATTERNS

I like crown patterns because they signal a new trend. I really love continuation patterns (as shown in Figure 12.8) because they keep the new trend going. This is when you let your profits run, enter a trend late because you

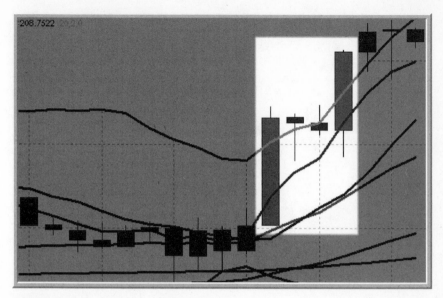

FIGURE 12.8 Continuation Pattern
Source: FX Bootcamp, LLC (www.fxbootcamp.com)
DealBook® 360 screen capture printed by permission. © 2008 by Global Forex Trading, Ada MI USA

did not spot the previous trend reversal, or if you are an advanced trader, when you can add additional lots.

Not only that, they are clear signs of where support levels are and suggest fantastic places to put or move stop losses. Price makes a new trend, retraces a bit, and then takes off again—continuation.

Look at these great examples. Notice that the continuation patterns and crown patterns work even on the weekly charts. Yes, they work on all time frames, not just intraday charts. This shows how powerful these candle formations are. Take a look at the weekly chart in Figure 12.9.

Can you see the crown pattern I've outlined above? This is a clear reversal signal. The chart is no longer forming lower lows and lower highs. The trend has been broken and momentum is now moving up. Now, let's watch what happens next in Figure 12.10.

You will see our crown at the bottom left corner. Look what then happened over and over again: continuation patterns! Notice the very strong trend of higher highs and higher lows. This trend continued for two years, and the end was signaled by another crown pattern. The reversal from a bull market to a bear market was obvious.

You should ride these continuation patterns until you see a reversal pattern. Remember, the trend is your friend. When you see a pause in the

FIGURE 12.9 Inverse Crown
Source: FX Bootcamp, LLC (www.fxbootcamp.com)
DealBook® 360 screen capture printed by permission. © 2008 by Global Forex
Trading, Ada MI USA

FIGURE 12.10 Inverse Crown Continuation
Source: FX Bootcamp, LLC (www.fxbootcamp.com)
DealBook® 360 screen capture printed by permission. © 2008 by Global Forex
Trading, Ada MI USA

trend, create trade plans that will put you into the trend when it shows signs of continuing.

Do not bet against the trend. This means price must stop making new highs/lows, the first signs of reversal, before even thinking of trading against the trend. Once you have a lower high or higher low, then you can plan for a reversal.

TRENDING ONLY

Candlesticks work great in a trending market. They are used in conjunction with other forms of technical analysis. They also work best at levels previously identified as support or resistance. This is an important point to remember, as candlesticks can help you see if a trend is running out of steam or not. They can also keep you in a trending trade.

Imagine if you were in a trend trade and you were profiting well. Nice! However, price is getting closer and closer to resistance. What do you do: Take profit or let it run? Let's wait and see.

Price hits the resistance. What happens? Was it riding the 5, 21, or 55? The faster the speed of the market, the more confident you should be that it will break resistance; however, you are still likely to see hesitation or pullback.

So it's riding the 21. It's a pretty good market, but it could be exhausting. Now look at the 55. How far is it from the 21? Wide angle and separation between the two shows more strength than flat and narrow. The more strength that appears in the 21/55, the more confident you should be that price will break through the resistance level.

Oh, so the speed of the market is looking like it is flattening? The distance between the 21/55 is diminishing? Your confidence of breaking above the resistance should wane.

Right at resistance, the next candle was a spinning top. No big deal; however, you were expecting price to respect the resistance level. You are worried about a reversal at this level. A spinning top doesn't add to or subtract from your confidence.

The third candle at the resistance level is big and red. On its own, it would be a bearish engulfing candle. This means it is very red and very big compared to the other candles around it. However, combined with the previous two candles, a reversal candlestick formation has formed: the evening star reversal pattern.

This is exactly the sort of evidence you were looking for: a reversal pattern at resistance while the market is slowing. You now have enough information to cash out of your bullish trade. You decide to take your profits and run.

SUMMARY

It wasn't just the candlestick formation that made you get out of your winning trade. It wasn't fear or any other emotion. You measured the strength of the market and were looking for signs of reversal. As soon as you saw evidence of such, you logically took profit. This is exactly how to use candlestick patterns.

In contrast, if the market was moving more quickly, such as riding the 5, things may have turned out differently.

You may have broken through resistance immediately. In this case, you often see a pullback, but resistance has become support and price blasts off like a rocket again. Notice that this actually created a continuation pattern.

In any case, you need a trend to continue or to reverse. What if you are not in a trend but caught in a range? We will explore this question in Chapter 13.

Range Trading

E ventually, all trends run out of steam. Price just gets too far from the 200 EMA and must return to its equilibrium point, as shown in Figure 13.1.

Price usually doesn't reverse quickly. In most situations the market exhausts. You can easily see the slow reversals previously discussed as an old man in a hot bath in Chapter 9 by watching the moving averages lose angle and separation. First, momentum will be lost and the 5/8 will braid. Then the 21/55 will flatten. Price eases in a new direction.

Then, as the market slows, the 200 EMA will catch up. Your medium-term analysis will be important here, as you do not know, at this time, if price will indeed reverse or if it will continue in the direction of the prevailing trend after it hits the 200 EMA.

In the meantime, you can range trade while you are in the exhaustion phase. This means you can trade between the bounces. Because the market lacks trend, price will likely be rejected at support and resistance levels.

Savvy traders can take short-term trades in this type of market, buying as support and selling at resistance until the market chooses direction, creating a new trending phase.

GET IN THE RING

Range trading is like prize fighting. In the green corner, you have the Bulls. In the red corner, you have the Bears. Both of the fighters are equally

FIGURE 13.1 Breakout Cycle
Source: FX Bootcamp, LLC (www.fxbootcamp.com)
DealBook® 360 screen capture printed by permission. © 2008 by Global Forex Trading, Ada MI USA

matched, however, the current champion (the prevailing trend) has the best odds of winning, but all champs retire at some point.

Range trading is a slugfest. Both fighters stand toe to toe, exchanging blows back and forth. It's going to be a long and bloody fight to the end. It's not going to be easy for either fighter.

In the case of forex range trading, you are betting on both traders. You are not necessarily concerned with who wins. Your wagers are on who will win each individual round. Each round is another opportunity to put money on the table.

FLOORS AND CEILINGS

Support and resistance is the name of the game. In range trading, you are assuming that they will not break. Your trading will be based on the assumption that the range will hold. Range traders want to short at the top and buy at the bottom.

The best tools for range trading indicate when a currency pair may be overbought and oversold. These technical indicators are called oscillators.

The oscillator we use the most at FX Bootcamp is the Stochastics. There are many others to choose from. The Relative Strength Index (RSI) is another popular oscillator.

The first step in range trading is to identify support and resistance. These price levels will be the floor and ceiling for price action while we are locked into the current range.

Because you are creating a trade plan based on selling at resistance and buying at support, you are looking for confirmation to do so. Just like any trade plan, you are not going to guess that price will respond to these levels. You are looking for evidence that support or resistance *did* hold. With evidence, you now have permission to consider a range trade.

The evidence you are looking for, after price is rejected at support or resistance, is a Stochastic cross. They are easy to spot, but some crosses are better than others. Stochastic crosses should be qualified by the oversold and overbought lines. See Figure 13.2.

OVER AND OUT

Notice the horizontal lines within the stochastic oscillator. The bottom line is placed at the 25 percent level. The bottom line is placed at the 75 percent level. Anytime the two lines are below the 25 percent level, price is

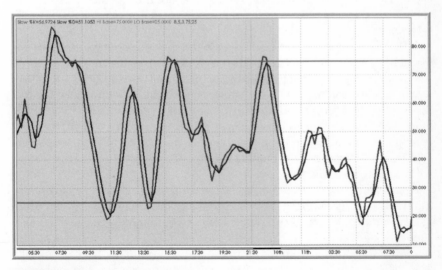

FIGURE 13.2 Stochastic Crosses
Source: DealBook® 360 screen capture printed by permission. © 2008 by Global Forex Trading, Ada MI USA

considered oversold. Anytime the two lines are above the 75 percent level, price is considered overbought.

Does this mean sell above 75 percent or buy below 25 percent? Absolutely not! If there is a strong trend in place, price will cross these levels. Of course the market is oversold in a down trend—everyone is selling, and of course the market is overbought in an uptrend—everyone is buying!

There are two things to consider:

1. There must be no trend in place. The market must be in a range.
2. It's when the two lines cross and return to the midrange between 25 percent and 75 percent that you want to take notice.

What you are looking for is a change in direction. You are expecting the direction change in price to occur at support and resistance. Your trade plan is to wait for price to challenge support and resistance, then look for an alert to pull the trigger.

As the currency pair bounces between these price levels, you will notice stochastics bouncing between the 25 percent and 75 percent lines. If price changes direction, you will see evidence of this with a stochastic cross.

However, stochastics, like most technical indicators, is lagging. It measures past price action not current price action. Therefore, the stochastic oscillator will cross after price rejection has occurred. This is an easy alert to see. However, let me remind you that it is not the stochastic cross that is important. It is the fact that the stochastic oscillator crossed after it was rejected at support or resistance.

This is the alert in your trade plan that indicates support or resistance has held and price may return to the other extreme of the range.

You can see in Figure 13.3, that support and resistance is identified with black horizontal lines. What you cannot see in the example is that the these levels had been important for two or three previous days. The resistance line is 114.89, just below the psychological level of 115.00. Support is found at 114.37. It had been resistance several times in the past couple of days even forming the shoulders in two different crown patterns. These were a likely area for bounces.

The test of resistance followed by a stochastic cross was a valid opportunity to consider shorting, as long as the market is ranging as it had been in this example. When you sell at resistance, your target is the next level of support. See Figure 13.4.

Price steps down from the 21 to the 55 and eventually back to the 200 EMA. This also happens to be very close to our support area. A range trader is looking for opportunities to exit his short trade for profit and consider going long.

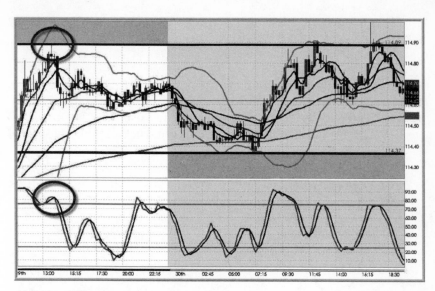

FIGURE 13.3 Support and Resistance
Source: FX Bootcamp, LLC (www.fxbootcamp.com)
DealBook® 360 screen capture printed by permission. © 2008 by Global Forex Trading, Ada MI USA

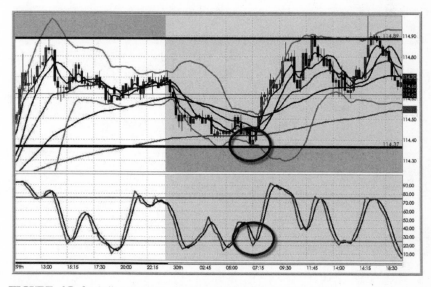

FIGURE 13.4 Sell at Resistance, Target Next Level of Support
Source: FX Bootcamp, LLC (www.fxbootcamp.com)
DealBook® 360 screen capture printed by permission. © 2008 by Global Forex Trading, Ada MI USA

A test of support and a stochastic cross would be a valid opportunity in a range bound market. Previous resistance is the next target.

Two points of caution to consider:

1. It is not as ideal to trade a stochastic cross if it is between 25 and 75 percent. The closer to 0 percent or 100 percent the better. Remember, an oscillator measures overbought and oversold. The more extreme the indicator reading the better. A cross in the middle may signal stagnation and braiding will begin on the 5/8.

2. To be even more conservative (and I am an extremely conservative trader), you can wait for price to cross at the stochastic extremes and then wait for the oscillator to return to the normal range of 25 to 75 percent. This will put you into your trades a bit later; however, it will help you avoid false signals.

As shown in Figure 13.5, two mistakes would have been made if you pulled the trigger.

1. Price got close to resistance, but did not touch it. If stochastics had confirmed, then maybe it could have been "close enough."

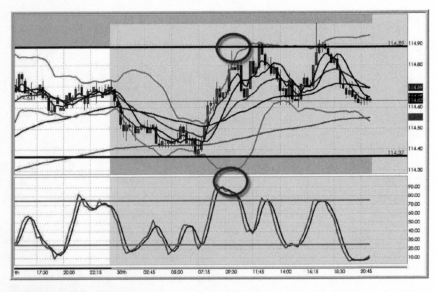

FIGURE 13.5 Caution
Source: FX Bootcamp, LLC (www.fxbootcamp.com)
DealBook® 360 screen capture printed by permission. © 2008 by Global Forex Trading, Ada MI USA

2. Stochastics had not dropped back below 75 percent. There was still buying pressure in the market that prevented the fall of price. The next test of resistance, 10 candles, was a better trade opportunity. In the end, it didn't yield much better results, but it did touch our resistance line and was confirmed by a proper stochastics cross. This trade ended up being knocked out at breakeven, so nothing was won or lost. This happens a lot in forex. Get used to it. But it was a more conservative trade.

SUMMARY

In the long run, you will be better off waiting for the more conservative trades. You may miss a few winning trades now and then, but you will also not be in a lot of losing trades. I'm happy to lose opportunity cost every so often from being conservative, rather than lose real money from being overly aggressive.

Being conservative doesn't always mean being passive or slow. It just means you have specific rules of engagement for various trade setups. You don't pull the trigger until those rules are met. In some cases, such as news trading, you can be "conservatively aggressive."

CHAPTER 14

Trading the News

I prefer trading with the trend. I love pulling the trigger when market and price are aligned. This makes minimal acceptable performance (MAP) much more likely. However, I often get lucky and price runs for quite some time after I've moved my stop to protect MAP. I seem to be unlucky more often when I'm trading against the trend.

However, even though currencies trend a lot, there are plenty of trading days when price stalls and we trade in a range for a few hours up to a few days. This means if we are going to trade, we need to adjust our expectations, become more conservative, and use the proper tools.

While range trading, I'm assuming that no luck will come my way, so I doubt we'll break out of the range. I'll use oscillators to buy at the bottom and sell at the top. I'll get in a little late and out a little late, but MAP is likely in between.

If your range is less than 30 pips, not only is your risk/reward ratio going to be poor, you are going to need to be a perfect trader to catch reasonable profit. Because I seek a 1:3 risk/reward ratio, I usually do not trade tight ranges. Although many traders have told me they do well in such cases, I have not. Trading the news has an entirely different set of risks associated with it. You must be very careful.

Let's first define what a "news trade" is and is not. In FX Bootcamp terms, it's a trade that attempts to capture volatility created by a news release. This volatility creates a "breakout trade" as price smashes through support or resistance.

When described with this definition, a news trade is *not* a trade that:

1. Is placed just before news is released.
2. Is placed just after news is released.

Please note: I do not place trades just before or after news.

Risky Business

What's wrong with those types of trading? Nothing is wrong with them, per say. Many traders claim to do well using various methods, such as "buy the rumor, sell the news" or "straddling" in which a trader places orders to buy and sell several pips away in hopes of catching the direction the news creates. I just don't prefer it.

At FX Bootcamp, our news trading strategy is to conservatively let undue volatility diminish before we trade. Why wait? It's too risky! There are several forms of risk unique to news trading.

- Spreads. Many brokers charge more for a trade right after news comes out. I've seen GBP/USD jump to a spread of 15 pips right after nonfarm payrolls. That is expensive!
- Slippage: Most brokers will have difficulty entering your order right after a news release, as they are flooded by thousands of orders in just a few seconds. This means your order could take longer to process and your trade could be entered many pips away from where you wanted.
- Stop jumping. An order, such as a stop loss working order needs to be touched by price before it is executed. However, sometimes after news is released, the market can jump several pips. For example, price could go from 115.50 to 115.65 instantly. It jumped! If your stop order was 115.60 you did not get stopped out. You are still in the market and exposed to potentially unlimited loses.
- Direction. Okay, this is not a risk only associated with news. Every time we pull the trigger, we face the risk of picking the wrong direction. However, those who place a trade just before the news comes out, in my humble opinion (humble because I am terrible with this type of strategy) they are reducing themselves to guessing the direction that will be created by the news.

Russian Roulette

There are many strategies for this type of before/after guess news trading, but I haven't found one I feel comfortable with. I work too hard to conservatively earn my pips throughout the month to risk any on a guess, even if the guess can pay off handsomely. It's too much like gambling.

Extreme example: Russian roulette. This is a high-stakes game. Two players challenge each other. One will live and one will die.

The rules are simple. A bullet is placed into an empty revolver so that all the chambers are unloaded but one. The cylinder is spun so one of chambers randomly loads the gun. Is the chamber empty or does it contain the bullet? No one knows.

The first player places the gun to his head and pulls the trigger ... "click" (hopefully); maybe he lives to continue playing the game—or not. If so, it is the next player's turn. They add another bullet, spin the cylinder and the second player places the gun to his head ... "click?"

As you can see, it's a "winner takes all" game of chance. Like forex, it is a zero-sum game. One player will win only because the other player lost. However, I don't feel comfortable with 50/50 odds: four loaded chambers and four empty. Now that is a game I would never like to play! That is exactly how I feel about betting on direction. If my odds are 50/50, I pass on the opportunity to trade. Like most Russian roulette players, I am too interested in surviving to enjoy the game.

Perfect Storm

Unfortunately, there are a lot of news events in the world of forex. Often, they disrupt the short-term market. Some people try to take advantage of this disruption, while I try to tiptoe around it.

I found, over a period of years trading forex, that many of the risks associated with news trades hit me all at once. This is because some news events disrupt more than others do.

Quarterly reports just carry more weight than monthly and weekly reports. Or sometimes, the results of a fundamental announcement are very surprising and shock the market for a while. In any case, a perfect storm can always be brewing, and it can be deadly.

Theoretical example: nonfarm payrolls. This announcement has been averaging 99 pips moves over the last two years for the EUR/USD. About half of these pips occur in the first two minutes. The worst-case scenario for a news trader would be:

1. The announcement comes out better than expected for the USD. A news trader immediately sells the EUR/USD currency pair (selling EUR/buying USD), just a second or two after the news becomes public. However, EUR/USD had already dropped 30 pips because of the pre-news guessers.

2. The broker gets thousands of similar sell orders at the exact same moment you sold the pair. It takes your broker a few seconds to execute the order. In the meantime, the EUR/USD has fallen another 15 pips while you wait.

3. Because volatility is so extreme to the downside (very few traders are placing buy orders) the broker widens the spread from three pips to nine pips.

4. The moment the order hits the market, the news trader is –9 pips, but also 45 from where he hoped the order would be.

5. Suddenly, the EUR/USD starts to pull all the way back to the start. Just seconds after the trader pulled the trigger, the trade is now –55 pips and the trader exits for a quick loss.

6. Angry about the loss, the trader blames the broker. The trader calls the broker, upset that the slow execution was the reason he lost money. The broker says, "Check your account agreement. We do not guarantee order execution at times of high volatility."

Is it really the broker's fault? No. I don't think so. Do news trades always end up this way? No. Not in my experience. But they can and do behave this way fairly often, depending on the importance or surprise results of the economic announcement. Therefore, I have developed a survival strategy to cover my ass.

CONSERVATIVE NEWS TRADES

First, let's review the three standing orders.

- Capital preservation: Survive at all costs.
- Capital acquisition: Lock in MAP.
- Capital appreciation: Go for maximum pips.

I review these now for you to align your satellites with the overall objective: Do all that you can to not lose money. The priority is not to make as much money as possible. It is to reduce your risk by patiently waiting for conservative, repeatable setups. News trading puts a trader's patience to the test. The object of the FX Bootcamp news trade is to use the undue volatility to identify the important levels of support and resistance.

After the results of economic announcements hit the news wires, the market often jumps. When it does, it blows through the nearest and weakest levels of support and resistance. However, at some point, price has jumped too far too fast and pulls back. This price level is very important

It often takes three to five minutes to reach this level. When price begins to pull back, I mark the end of the news spike with a horizontal line on the charts. Now it is easy to see, and we can create a trade plan.

Before we do so, let's review what happened.

Just before the news came out, the market began to wake up. Some traders are placing orders on hunches, rumors, or guesses. Remember, they can't know the results of the news before it is released.

However, sometimes this last-second volatility is created by traders exiting a trade before the news comes out, so the market may move in the wrong direction. Don't trade just because you see the market moving in a particular direction 20 seconds before the news announced.

In any case, don't pull the trigger yet. Win nothing. Lose nothing. Capital preservation at its best!

The news is then released and the market moves dramatically. Thousands of orders are placed. I still don't recommend trading because of the unique risks already explained, like slippage, gapping, spreads, and such. However, we have just gathered two pieces of intelligence to help us formulate a strategy.

1. We now know the results of the economic announcement. We know if it was good, bad, or a surprise. We use this information to formulate a long-term fundamental bias.

2. We also have clear evidence of market direction. Did the market jump up or down? For the short-term, we only want to trade in that direction. If price reverses in the next 15 to 30 minutes, ignore it.

For the next couple of minutes you are going to see relatively big candles; lots of green or red. Let the market move. Stay out. This is when discipline is so important. You'll want to jump in. Don't. It may feel like you are missing a trade opportunity; however, the only thing you are missing is risk.

In the meantime, you have a few minutes that you can either do some analysis with results of the economic report (what happened last time the results were similar to today's results), or you can simply wait a minute or two for a pullback.

Once price begins to pull back, you will have a better market to trade in. Volatility will still be high, but not wild, crazy, and out of control. Now slippage risk drops to virtually zero and spreads return to normal. Even better, you now know direction, support and resistance. You also have given yourself a few minutes to develop a trade plan based on how the market is behaving. No guesses!

Line in the Sand

Once price starts to pull back, you draw your horizontal line—what I call our line in the sand (see Figure 14.1). It's a clear threshold on a one-, three-, or five-minute chart. In most cases, you'll have a line on your chart near the three-minute post-news mark. Once drawn, you have to decide if you want to be aggressive or conservative with your trade entry.

How do you decide? It usually comes down to what the news results were. If they were a big surprise, maybe you will be more aggressive with your trade plan. If it's about as expected then perhaps you'll be more conservative. In any case, it's a judgment call you will have to make.

A Sniper Trade

Although I say this is a more aggressive entry, it is still a conservative trade because you are basing it on market intelligence and price behavior. Your plan is clear: Trade in the direction the market jumped after the news. You

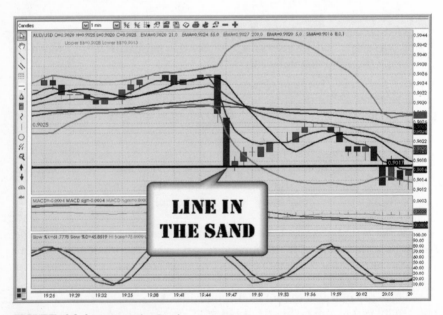

FIGURE 14.1 Line in the Sand
Source: FX Bootcamp, LLC (www.fxbootcamp.com) DealBook® 360 screen capture printed by permission. © 2008 by Global Forex Trading, Ada MI USA

are not terribly concerned with the line in the sand. You are planning to break it anyway.

Your strategy will be to enter a trade on the pullback (see Figure 14.2). Price almost always pulls back. These price retracements are often where amateur traders take losses. Therefore, the first benefit of this trade plan is that you are not in the trade during the pullback.

I call this a "sniper trade" because you know exactly what your target is (the line in the sand), and you are going to fire at it from a distance. If the news pushes price up, you are waiting a few minutes for price to drop before you enter a long trade. If the news pushes price down, you are waiting a few minutes for price to rise before you enter your short trade.

Either way, you are looking for signs that price has pulled back and then wants to return in the direction it had moved after the news came out. The pullback represents the rifle being loaded. After the pullback is complete and price continues in the post-news direction (this is really just a simple continuation pattern consisting of a pullback and extension) pull the trigger.

I consider this type of trade aggressive only because you are trading before the line in the sand has been crossed. However, it is only aggressive for my conservative trading style. In reality, it really is still quite a

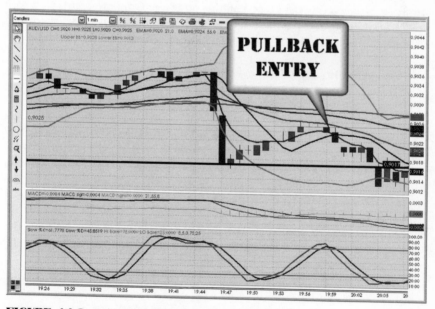

FIGURE 14.2 Pullback Entry
Source: FX Bootcamp, LLC (www.fxbootcamp.com) DealBook® 360 screen capture printed by permission. © 2008 by Global Forex Trading, Ada MI USA

conservative trade setup as it aims, first and foremost, to reduce risk before pulling the trigger.

Lock and Load

How far will it retrace before you pull the trigger and lock in your trade? You never know in advance. However, you are looking for evidence that the pullback was rejected. You are not going to guess. It seems that every time I guess, I lose. This is why I stopped guessing a long time ago.

However, as I said, I call this a sniper trade because before you fire a shotgun, you have to pull back the pump handle to get the weapon loaded. You are then going to fire from a distance. It's exactly the same thing with this type of news trade. You may be aiming up, but before you pull the trigger, the trade must be loaded with the pullback.

Rubber Bands

The moving averages and Bollinger bands are often places where price bounces as it retraces and then returns in the direction of your horizontal line. If news moved the market upward, then we are looking to go long.

Price, however, has already hit resistance and is now falling. After the news, you saw a few big green candles on the one-minute chart. Now you see a couple big red candles. Where will the candles likely start to turn green again? In this order, you will be looking for signs of a bounce at:

- The upper Bollinger band.
- The 5/8.
- The 21/55.

Somewhere in that mess of lines, price is likely to be supported. Why? Because there are many traders still waiting to go long, just like you.

After the red candles dissipate and you start to see green candles, you may consider going long for a sniper trade. Ideally, this occurs right on top of one of these lines. If it does, it will probably build your confidence, as it will seem to make sense.

For example, if you were watching a five-minute chart, and after the news and the close of the candle you were left with a big green candle, your plan would be to wait for a pull back before you go long.

Often after big news events, a candle like this will be way outside the normal deviation of price. It would be way above the Bollinger bands. If price then pulls back to the upper Bollinger band, you would see red candles on a one- or three-minute chart. As soon as you see green after a bounce on a Bollinger band or perhaps just below that on the five EMA, you can consider going long for your semi-aggressive sniper news trade.

Fibonacci Rally

Another great place to watch for a pullback bounce will be Fibonacci retracement levels. All you have to do is measure the distance from the pre-news candle to the horizontal line.

A Fib study will show you retracement levels (as shown in Figure 12.8). In the retracement zone a bounce will likely occur between 38.2 percent and 61.8 percent. If price falls into this Fib zone and then bounces, you will have an opportunity to consider sniper news trading.

Another upside of trading a rally at a Fibonacci retracement level is that it will also help you with a profit target. For example, a 61.8 percent retracement will often produce a 138.2 percent extension. See Figure 14.3.

Bayonet Trades

Waiting for support or resistance to be broken is a more conservative news trade strategy because you are waiting for a lower low or a higher high. You are not hoping it will break; you are waiting for it to break.

In the end, it is still a simple breakout pattern above post-news resistance or below post-news support. However, you are not entering before the break but after the break.

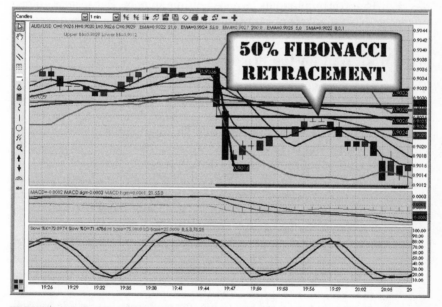

FIGURE 14.3 Fibonacci Pullback
Source: FX Bootcamp, LLC (www.fxbootcamp.com) DealBook® 360 screen capture printed by permission. © 2008 by Global Forex Trading, Ada MI USA

So, it may be the same trade opportunity as the sniper trade, however it is not from a distance, but close quarters combat. A bayonet is a specially designed knife that attaches to the end of a rifle. This means you are going to engage in hand-to-hand, face-to-face combat.

Charge the Line

In this strategy, you are going to engage after a break in the line. You are hoping there are enough traders willing to charge the line. They are going to plunge their bayonets into support/resistance. Remember, this is the defensive area that held the news spike.

If the line breaks, you keep moving forward.

In military strategy, when the enemy's line breaks and they retreat, they are at their most vulnerable. Pull the trigger as they pull back. You will advance quickly as you rout them.

Once they regroup, new support and resistance will hold. If the news is big, then we'll overwhelm them as some of their troops will either desert or convert to our side. In such situations, a continuation pattern will form and we'll go to the next line of defense. We'll do this over and over until both sides exhaust.

If the line does not break with our post-news assault, well, then you've lost your trade opportunity and you should retreat and live to trade another day. However, this will result in a loss of our snipers. Because we didn't break the line, we left them exposed and the pullback became a reversal.

Wait, Wait, Wait for the Break

This trade is very conservative. The idea is to let news come out, let the volatility identify support or resistance, let price pull back, let price bounce, and then let price break the horizontal line in the sand. It's simply a breakout trade following a continuation pattern created by the news release. See Figure 14.4.

That is a lot of waiting! It takes patience, but it will also keep you out of a lot of bad trades. If the market is reacting powerfully to the news, then this type of trade often works. However, if the results of the fundamental economic announcement were mixed, then the trade doesn't fully form, and you end up not trading at all.

In this case, capital preservation wins again. However, if executed, your trade was based on a repeatable pattern (continuation pattern) in the logical direction of the fundamental announcement. Even if the trade doesn't work out, you won't feel stupid about it.

This is important, as you need to log this trade into your trade journal. Your journal is like a courtmartial. Will you have a good case when you

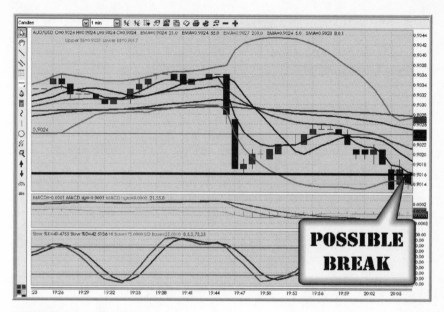

FIGURE 14.4 Possible Breakout
Source: FX Bootcamp, LLC (www.fxbootcamp.com) DealBook® 360 screen capture printed by permission. © 2008 by Global Forex Trading, Ada MI USA

explain why you pulled the trigger? Were your actions justifiable? Will you plead insanity? Why did you give the order?

More or Less Conservative

The pullback trade is conservative. The breakout trade is more conservative. Both are conservative because in either case, you do not face as many news-trade-associated risks as you would trading just before or after the fundamental announcement.

Not only that, you are not in the trade early and stressing while price pulls back and perhaps forcing you to exit the trade for a loss. You haven't pulled the trigger before the pullback! Isn't that wonderful? You are still setting a trap.

With the sniper trade, you use the pullback to identify your target and fire at it from a distance. In the bayonet trade, you are waiting for a continuation beyond support/resistance before you trade. Either way, you let the undue volatility created by the news identify support or resistance. Then, based on your fundamental analysis of the news results, you decide to trade before price breaks beyond the line in the sand, or after.

Easy, right? For some reason, it's not easy to learn. It does not matter if you are news, scalping, spot, swing, carry, or position trading, your success will come with planning your trades in advance. Think of it this way: Don't fight on a level playing field.

Take the High Ground

In war, it is best to take the high ground and build fortifications. After you have done this, all you have to do is wait for the enemy to attack you. If they do, you will certainly have the upper hand.

If the enemy does not attack you, do *not* meet them on a level playing field where you do not have a tactical advantage. If the enemy does not fall for your trap, don't attack. If they leave, you will simply leave, too, and set another trap somewhere else.

This means that your chance of survival is much higher. You are not looking for a fight. Your primary goal is simply to survive. If you are attacked, you want the best odds of surviving. If you are not attacked, then you automatically survive as you avoided confrontation.

"War does not determine who is right—only who is left."
—Bertrand Russell

Set your trap after the pullback has begun. In a long trade scenario, let price fall after it has identified resistance for you. If it falls and never comes back, then it has reversed. Don't do anything. You are not planning a reversal trade.

By taking the high ground and planning a trade based on a pullback bounce or a support/resistance breakout, you put yourself in a trade with a high probability of success with lower news-trade-associated risks.

If you don't get either of these trade setups, then all you do is watch price reverse. It's like watching your enemy retreat after they see your fortification at the top of the hill. There simply will be no battle today. You are not in the reversal trade, so you are not making money, but hey, you are not losing money either. Just do some more analysis and create a new trade plan. There is always another trade. Set a trap for it. Find a new hill, build new fortifications, and wait for your enemy to attack you.

SUMMARY

A news trade is unique. It is separate from other types of trades that take into account speed of the markets, momentum of price, and the long-term trend. It's just a very short-term trade based on post-news volatility. You don't marry these trades—just love 'em and leave 'em.

Many of my news trades, if not most, break even. I quickly get up 10 or 20 pips, just to have price come back and knock me out. This happens because I quickly move my stop so I take all risk off the table. Often the trade results in nothing, but several times a week I get lucky and price continues in my favor.

There are probably 10 to 15 news trade opportunities every week. Let's say 10 of them break even and you earn zero pips. Let's say on three others you earn only 15 pips, getting knocked out on pullbacks after you lock in MAP. Then let's say twice you really get lucky and make 50 pips on the other two. It really does happen this way. Not every week, but many. You certainly could average daily MAP, or 75 pips per week, doing nothing but this type of trading.

However, trading this way is not likely to lead to the lifestyle or stress level you want for your career. But think of this news trading methodology this way. If you made an extra 75 pips a week on these short-term trades, they would offset one or two of your stupid trades. They could bring you closer to being a consistently profitable trader. Or at least get you to be a breakeven trader.

In any case, they could keep you trading longer so you can gain more experience and thereby become a more skilled trader. This is a positive cycle, and I hope it helps you get your trading to the next level or perhaps even to total success. But even with success, you still have the challenges that professional and novice traders both face: the psychological aspects of trading.

Technical and fundamental analysis are the basic skills all forex traders must have to understand how and why the market is behaving the way it is. However, trader psychology is much more important. There are many fantastic analysts who likely can't trade worth a hoot. Just ask yourself, how many times has your analysis been correct, but you still lost money? I believe the true secret to success is not just learning how to trade but learning how to be a successful trader.

PART FOUR SUMMARY

To recap, following are the key takeaways for Part Four:

- Candlesticks are signs of trader behavior.
- Some candlesticks appear on their own.
- Others join together to form patterns.
- Doji and spinning tops show exhaustion.

- Combined with other larger candles, they can form star reversal patterns.
- Top and crown patterns are also reversal signs.
- Such patterns need a strong trend behind them or there is nothing to reverse.
- Candles can also show trend continuation.
- The key to continuation or reversals is support and resistance.
- Price often breaks, rallies, exhausts, and then reverses over time.
- To measure price action vs. support or resistance, use an oscillator.
- Divergence and reversal patterns decrease the chances of a new breakout.
- News trading has unique risks associated with it. It is best to avoid trading just before or after the news is released.
- Use the news spike to identify a line in the sand to use in your news trading.
- Ignore news-trade-related reversals.
- The bigger the news results, the more aggressive your trade plan can be.
- You may conservatively trade breakouts.
- You may aggressively trade news pullbacks.
- Pullbacks often return at Bollinger bands, moving averages or Fibonacci levels.
- Watch at least two time frames, such as a 15-minute and a 1-minute chart.

Psychological Warfare

I n the following chapters, you will learn much more than technical or fundamental analysis. You will learn about yourself and how you trade.

Stress is a risk that you must manage if you are going to be a successful trader over a long period of time. To be able to last in this business, you are going to have to focus on improving your trading skills each day and focus on your trading goals years in advance.

Part Five focuses on the psychology of trading, your place in the forex market, and how you can adapt to survive. Your entrepreneurial skills brought you to forex, however those skills will lead to your downfall if you do not learn how to harness that energy.

In Part Five, you will learn:

- How to understand your own trading.
- How retail traders fit in the market.
- How professional traders fit in the market.
- How you can use the pros as your guide.
- How to manage the risk of stress.
- How to manage the risk of money.
- How to keep a trade journal.

- How to use a trade journal properly.
- How to improve your trading skills.
- How to plan your trading like a business.
- How to budget your trading long-term.
- How to survive, grow, and prosper.

CHAPTER 15

How to Cope with Pre- and Post-Trading Stress Disorders

Trading forex is not easy. In fact, it can be downright difficult at times. This is not due to charts or indicators. Mastering fundamental and technical analysis will help, but they are not the keys to success. Why not? In a word: humanity.

Forex is not about red candles and green candles. It's about the traders who are creating them. Their greed and fear are represented by the colors on your charts. That means there are times that logic simply fails.

This makes forex a challenge to master. Recently, during a trip to Tokyo, after my presentation to a group of forex traders, I hung out with a couple of the attendees. One of them was an astrophysicist who had become a banker. As vice president of the bank, he had only one task: build a computer that will help the bank's traders make trading decisions. Fun job, eh? I bet it pays better than NASA!

In any case, after a few pints of Guinness (isn't it amazing that you can find an Irish pub in virtually every city on the planet?) we discussed his progress building a virtual trader for the bank. This is a summarized version of the conversation.

"How does it work for equities?" I asked.

"Great."

"How does it work for bonds?"

"Amazing."

"Commodities?"

"You bet."

"How about currencies?"

"Can't be done."

187

"What?"

"The market is too liquid, too efficient, and often too volatile. We simply can't model the market. Sometimes the system works great. Other times, not at all."

It's amazing what you can learn if you just ask. I guess that is why he was at my presentation about forex trading. He wanted to learn more about successful forex traders, perhaps to mimic them in his computer model.

It reminded me of a famous quote.

Reporter: "Mr. Gandhi, what do you think of Western civilization?"
Mahatma Gandhi: "I think it is a good idea."

I think a computer that trades for me 24 hours a day and makes me filthy, stinking, and wonderfully rich is a good idea. Until that dream becomes a reality, I'll have to work to earn my daily bread.

My presentation, like this book, was about planning your trades several candles out before you pull the trigger. I'd guess that his computer models failed on the long-term because the computer was reacting to the market. It cannot think ahead like we can.

A computer just doesn't understand greed and fear. If forex was dominated by automated computer trading, then we'd have a much different forex market. As is, we need to understand forex by seeing the humanity in our charts.

How do we do this? Look into ourselves. Our success and failure is within us. It's in our hearts, minds, and souls. The key to forex is in the grey matter sitting between our ears and behind our eyes. It's a mind game!

GOING MENTAL

You must first fully master fundamental and technical analysis. Do not forget that. You must have these basic skills.

Having talked to amateur traders all over the world, I find that most traders with six months of experience are pretty good at technical analysis. Often they have purchased a couple of books and DVDs, or perhaps even a few PDFs off of eBay auctions (www.ebay.com/fxbootcamp is our link). They have found tons of great, and often free, resources such as live webinars at FXstreet.com. In any case, most new traders have made some effort to educate themselves. However, they still are not finding success. Why?

Were the books, videos, and expert webinars wrong? Not likely. The missing pieces are psychological and emotional. That is one reason why FX

Bootcamp is so powerful. It's live and we can discuss this aspect of trading on a daily basis; it's human to human interaction. A DVD or book simply can't do that. Books and videos can teach you how to do the analysis; only another trader can teach you how to trade.

COMMON THREAD

We have something in common; we are both a little bit crazy to trade forex.

I'm sure if you stood on the corner of a busy street and asked everyone who passed by if they were interested in putting money in one of the riskiest financial markets on the planet, they'd laugh and say, "No way, Jose!"

Most people are sane. They like going to their 9 to 5 jobs. They like their secure paychecks. It's steady and reliable. All they have to do is lay low in their cubicals and attend a few meetings. This makes them appear busy and helps them to get through the day. It may seem to be guaranteed poverty to risk takers like us, but to them, it's risk free and they like it.

Sane people run from risk. Not you and me. For some reason we are attracted to it. This is the entrepreneur inside us. It's our common thread. We have a high tolerance for risk, and we like the potential of big rewards. It's also our greatest downfall!

Our entrepreneurial spirit attracted us to forex. Now you must learn how to harness, shape, and mold that energy. If you don't, it will lead you to your doom. Forex isn't about assuming risk. Success comes with the management of risk.

Think of it this way. Hedge fund managers, central bankers, and corporate financial officers are the people who control the forex market. Not small retail traders like us. We are entrepreneurial. They are not. Their personalities are quite the opposite. Those guys are number crunchers, bean counters, and financial geniuses. They are extremely educated, likely at the best schools on the planet.

Money to them is an abstract. They think about forex and trade forex much differently from you and I, as they trade other people's money. Trading is not personal for them. Not to mention, they draw a big fat salary, and so their daily motivations are quite different from traders without a salary who risk their own money.

For most of these traders, forex is not fun. It's not liberation from their 9 to 5 job. It *is* their 9 to 5 job. They make trades that create the market. Forex is all about numbers to them. They don't have an entrepreneurial bone in their bodies. All they care about is return on investment.

It's only business to them. They have more money than you, more resources than you and, if they can, they will crush you and take your money.

If they lose some money on a bad trade, no big deal. It's not their money they've lost. They still get their salary.

Imagine all the traders in the banks that invested in subprime mortgages and lost billions of dollars. Hopefully many of them got fired. But I'm sure they all still live in huge houses, drive fancy cars, and live like royalty.

If you lost big money trading forex, you would feel the loss and it would hurt. The blood and tears are yours.

Monkey Business

In any case, professional traders are like 800-pound gorillas. They climb the trees and grab all the bananas. However, they can get fat and lazy.

Retail traders are like little monkeys. We shouldn't climb the trees. The gorillas may hurt us. We should wait for them to drop the bananas, and then we can sneak in and grab them before they notice. We need to be quick and nimble.

Let the gorillas do all the hard work. We can live off their lost spoils. Remember, if you challenge them, you will be crushed.

Follow the Leader

Sometimes logic fails in forex.

On November 2, 2007, I did a three-hour live trading webinar at FXstreet.com, covering the nonfarm payrolls (NFP) economic announcement. The headline number was 166,000 jobs added to the economy the previous month, much better than the 80,000 that was expected. Logic would dictate that the USD would gain strength on such positive news. It didn't. In fact, within 15 minutes, it was losing value (as shown in Figure 15.1).

Why does this happen?

The gorillas can do this to us. Remember, they have different goals than we do. Even though the market should fall on the great USD news, long-term professionals who see more USD weakness in the coming years, simply do the opposite; instead of selling EUR/USD, they buy it

My guess is that a lot of retail traders saw the great headline NFP number and instantly shorted the EUR/USD. As you can see, their logic may be correct, but it was a losing trade.

Price dropped 50 pips and then shot up 75 pips. However, price crashed so fast, I'm sure most traders who did short, got their trade in near the bottom, which means the sudden rise of 75 pips would have provided a huge loss to most who shorted, even though it was logical that they did.

Employing the wait-five-minutes-to-identify-support-and-resistance-pullback strategies outlined earlier in this book, we did not get a trade opportunity. We did not pull the trigger on the EUR/USD. We made no pips. However, I'm very happy to say that we did not lose any either. Capital

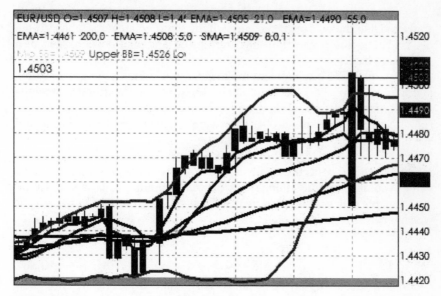

FIGURE 15.1 Figure 15.1 Nonfarm Payrolls Economic Announcement
Source: FX Bootcamp, LLC (www.fxbootcamp.com)
DealBook® 360 screen capture printed by permission. © 2008 by Global Forex Trading, Ada MI USA

preservation was the overall theme for that NFP. We survived to trade another day when things are not so risky.

The message here is to not just jump in because the news was good or bad. There are a lot of big players in this market that will make trades based on an entirely different set of criteria than you and I use. We may be thinking hours ahead and the professional traders who control the market are thinking months or years ahead. They will roll over you if you are in their way.

The 800-pound gorillas control the market. Let them be the leaders. Don't fight them. Let them lead. Let them show you the direction they want to go—and follow, survive and, if you can, try to pick up a few bananas along the way!

UNDERSTAND YOURSELF, UNDERSTAND YOUR TRADES

Even though understanding the humanity in the charts is important, understanding yourself is even more vital to your success. To understand the market's greed and fear, you must first understand your own.

There comes a time where all new forex traders have to search their souls and ask themselves if they are willing to do whatever it takes to succeed. I think this is an important step in the personal development of a successful trader.

There needs to be a moment in time that you mentally commit to forex. Many trade simply because it is fun and exciting. Having attended so many forex conferences around the world, it seems like the vast majority of new traders are just checking it out. They want to "play forex" for a while and see how it goes.

However, because you bought this book, you are likely a lot more serious than that. This is especially true if you have been trading forex for a while. You are probably doing okay. So what's holding you back from unquestionable success? It could be you. I can say this, because in my case, it was me who was holding me back.

Mano y Mano

I had to confront myself in the mirror. I looked myself in the eyes and asked:

- Do I have the guts to push myself to the next level?
- Am I willing to do whatever it takes to find success?

This may seem silly. However, I assure you, it was an important step for me. I "reenlisted" in forex and made a 100 percent total commitment.

I realized that success in forex was a lot more than making winning trades. It was striving for greatness. To be a great trader requires an unbelievable amount of work, energy, and effort. It requires patience and discipline well beyond what 95 percent of the market is willing or capable of doing. I realized that if I wanted to be in the top 5 percent of the market, I had to act like I was. I had to strive to be the perfect trader.

Born to Trade

No one was "born to trade." No one can be a perfect trader, but you can try.

Because I had no one to coach me and teach me how to trade forex successfully, I had to create the perfect trader and make that mythical trader my trading coach.

My idea was to identify what characteristics a perfect trader would have and pretend I could live up to those standards. My goal was to keep pretending until I forgot I was pretending.

My energy was then focused on developing positive trading habits and not on making money. It changed my entire outlook on forex. I was focused on the long-term aspects of my trading skills and my trading career. However, I soon came to realize it was going to take a lot of effort.

I started by creating a list of things I thought a perfect trader would be doing.

- Keep a trade journal.
- Review my trades.
- Understand my strengths and weaknesses.
- Work on specific trading goals.
- Manage my risk.
- Plan my trading business.
- Practice conservative and repeatable trading.
- Commit 100 percent or walk away from a trade.

With my list in hand, I then started to experiment with various ways of incorporating these habits into my trading career. Although I knew the vision of a perfect trader was a mirage, I was still certain that working toward developing positive trading habits could only lead me on a path toward success. The journey would be a positive experience.

Forex is a zero-sum game. If I lose, someone else has won. Therefore, it seemed that if most novice traders wouldn't do all this stuff, then perhaps I'd deserve success if I just outworked the other guy.

My goal was now clear. Put all my energy into doing what the trader on the other side of my trade is simply not willing to do. I'll work harder. I'll work smarter. I'll do more research. I'll wait for better entries. Most importantly, if I haven't done the work to set up a trade, I'll have the guts to *not* trade, to never react to price action, to only trade my plans. This will take patience. This will take discipline. This will need a 100 percent commitment.

Looking into the mirror, I made that 100 percent commitment to forex. It was my first step in becoming a professional forex trader. I was not born to trade, so perhaps I can never become the perfect trader. But I can keep trying.

SUMMARY

The surest way to find success in forex trading is to set goals and recognize your own strengths and limitations as a trader. Because no one is born to trade, traders must hone their craft through self-reflection, study, and practice. While this book will provide you with the tools to make smart trading decisions, it is up to you to take the extra steps to become a great trader. The next few chapters will discuss ways that you can improve and track your trades while constantly setting new targets.

CHAPTER 16

Trade Journals

T rade journals are extremely important to new traders. They play an important role in the development and refinement of a trader's skill. Unfortunately, most traders don't keep a journal. Even worse, those who do keep a trade journal often don't use them properly.

There is more to a journal than just trade data. Entering your price in, price out, and profit/loss is not the point of a trade journal. Your trading platform already has that data automatically captured for you. This data is important financial data, but it won't make you a better trader. See Figure 16.1.

The secret to a trade journal is your mind. Your mind does not know the difference between a thought and reality.

Your mind simply processes electrical-chemical energy. The energy stored in your brain can be from a memory of a past trade. It can also be from visual input from an outward sense, such as chart images seen with your eyes.

The images get converted into electrical-chemical energy—the same as a memory. To your mind, there is very little difference between your last trade and the trade you are in now. They are both just electrical-chemical energy. Both are real.

This can work for you. If you keep and use a trade journal properly, you will gain at least three years of trading experience for every 12 months that you actually trade forex. This means you can quickly become a much better trader than the vast majority of other novice traders and hopefully be on the winning side of their losing trades. But you have to work for it. You have to earn your success.

	Date	Type	Lots	Size	Pair	Price In	Price Out	PIP	P/L	Entry	Exit
☐	9/19/2006	Buy	1	Standard	EUR/USD	1.2689	1.2713	24	Profit	Good	Good
☐	9/20/2006	Buy	1	Standard	EUR/USD	1.2685	1.2687	2	Profit	Early	Early
☐	9/21/2006	Sell	2	Standard	GBP/USD	1.898	1.8965	15	Profit	Good	Late
☐	9/21/2006	Buy	2	Standard	GBP/USD	1.8979	1.9016	37	Profit	Good	Good
☐	9/22/2006	Sell	2	Standard	GBP/USD	1.1921	1.1941	20	Loss	Early	Early
☐	9/22/2006	Sell	2	Standard	EUR/USD	1.2816	1.2807	9	Profit	Early	Early
☐	9/25/2006	Sell	2	Standard	EUR/USD	1.2762	1.2742	20	Profit	Early	Early
☐	9/26/2006	Buy	2	Standard	EUR/USD	1.2701	1.269	11	Loss	Early	Good
☐	9/28/2006	Sell	7	Standard	EUR/USD	1.2698	1.2686	12	Profit	Good	Good
☐	9/29/2006	Buy	2	Standard	EUR/USD	1.2661	1.2646	15	Loss	Early	Early
☐	10/2/2006	Sell	1	Standard	EUR/USD	1.2685	1.2695	10	Loss	Early	Early
☐	10/2/2006	Buy	2	Standard	GBP/USD	1.8725	1.876	35	Profit	Good	Good
☐	10/2/2006	Buy	2	Standard	EUR/USD	1.27	1.2735	35	Profit	Good	Good
☐	10/2/2006	Sell	1	Standard	EUR/USD	1.274	1.275	10	Loss	Good	Early
☐	10/3/2006	Buy	2	Standard	EUR/USD	1.2739	1.2729	10	Loss	Early	Early
☐	10/4/2006	Buy	2	Standard	GBP/USD	1.8801	1.881	9	Profit	Early	Late
☐	10/4/2006	Buy	2	Standard	GBP/USD	1.8819	1.8832	13	Profit	Late	Early
☐	10/5/2006	Sell	2	Standard	EUR/USD	1.2687	1.2695	8	Loss	Late	Early
☐	10/5/2006	Buy	2	Standard	EUR/USD	1.2688	1.2676	12	Loss	Late	Late
☐	10/6/2006	Sell	2	Standard	GBP/USD	1.8737	1.8717	20	Profit	Late	Good
☐	10/6/2006	Sell	2	Standard	EUR/USD	1.2597	1.259	7	Profit	Late	Good
☐	11/1/2007	Sell	2	Standard	GBP/USD	2.4000	2.2000	100	Profit	Good	Good

FIGURE 16.1 Journal Data
Source: FX Bootcamp, LLC (www.fxbootcamp.com)

Elements of a Good Trade Journal

The secret to learning how to trade forex is exactly the same as achieving success at playing the piano, golf, chess, or developing any other skill. You work your butt off until you get really good at what you do. There is no other way to succeed. Stop looking for the secret formula, indicator, or alert service. They don't exist. They are fool's gold.

Trade journals require a three-step process:

1. The first step is to wait for conservative and repeatable trades. Set them up in advance with trade plans. If you miss a trade, just walk away and create a new plan. If you get a trade setup that you planned for, you must trade your plan. You strive to become able to trade like the perfect trader.

   This is hard work. It will make you pull the trigger a lot less, but your win/loss ratio will improve. You may miss a few winning trades now and then, but you'll miss far more bad trades that you would have taken in the past when simply reacting to the market.

2. The second step is to document all your trades. Each and every trade goes into your trade journal. This will take a lot of time.

   a. You must log your critical financial data, such as price in/out and profit/loss. However, a trade journal is much more than that.

    b. You should also include your reasoning for getting in and out of the trade. Document as much detail as you can about your mind-set while in the heat of the moment. The more you can tell yourself, the more you will learn from yourself.

    c. An image of your charts is also necessary. Save a screenshot of your trade just after you exit. This image will hold a visual record of your entry and exit. It will assist you in trying to relive your trade later.

3. Weekly review of your trades. This is the step that most traders, who actually keep a trade journal, skip. However, I think it is the main reason to keep a journal. How much can you really learn from your profit/loss statement?

    The goal here is to identify your strengths and weaknesses. If, for example, your entries seem to be late or your exits are early, perhaps you should be working on improving them.

It all comes down to your trading, but if you are going to improve your trading, you must strive to get better. Ideally, you are wrapped in blinders and focusing only on trade planning, not on making money.

The more you pretend to be a perfect trader, the closer you actually become to being a perfect trader. For me, the discipline became a game. If I missed a trade and saw a huge candle, I was extremely tempted to jump in. However, I knew the perfect trader would not. Perfect traders always plan their trades and trade their plans. That's it, nothing else. Don't be tempted into chasing price.

A Mind Game

So learning how to conservatively plan my trading became a game. Did I have what it takes to not trade? Could I manage my emotions? At first, I resorted to walking away from my keyboard for a few minutes. Taping your hands to your desk, tying and untying knots in your shoelaces, or other such distractions work equally well.

Over time, I got better at not jumping in. I'd simply say, "Wow! Look at that big candle! How come I didn't see that coming?" This survival skill didn't come quickly, but it was an important setup in my development as a trader.

Over time, I began to miss fewer and fewer trades. I began to find trades that I could recognize, and I began to spot them over and over again. For example, I found myself trading 5/8 crosses after a bounce at a reversal pivot point. For some reason, I found them easy to see and traded them a lot.

Then, as I gained more experience trading, I started seeing other trade setups, such as pullbacks to moving averages and candlestick patterns. Then I experimented with various time frames, such as four-hour charts.

This additional experience helped me add more repeatable trades to my repertoire. I just got better and better at spotting trade setups. This is because I recognized what the market was doing and traded it. If my plan was wrong, I didn't trade. I only traded on my terms on my turf.

It was only natural that I got better. It wasn't from making a lot of trades. Trading didn't provide the experience I needed to succeed. Planning trades did. Planning trades became a skill. However, it was my willingness to stick to my plans and trade nothing else that was the key to my success. I was able to trade what came naturally to me, then slowly get better and better. I then began to trade confidently.

Natural Born Traders

Was I a natural born trader? Hardly! I had the worst instincts and my gut feeling was always wrong. I think I was born the world's worst trader. However, my trade journal improved my trading right away.

I documented every trade in my trade journal. I would grab a screenshot of my trade and then enter it into the journal, which was an Excel spreadsheet. After entering all my financial data, I would insert long and detailed notes of why and how I made the trade.

This forced me to think about it. Why did I take the trade? What justified the risk? Why did I get out? This allowed me to relive each of my trades.

Remember, your mind does not know the difference between your last trade and your current trade. To your mind, both are real and in the moment. Just thinking about the details of my trades was like making the trade all over again. My trade journal doubled my trade experience instantly.

I really needed this experience as well. I needed to get past my lousy feel for the market. I needed more control, and I achieved this by planning my trades. Then, by reviewing my trades, I learned from each of my wins and each of my losses.

The trade journal then became a check and balance. I found that if I wasn't certain about the trade setup, I didn't make the trade because I didn't want to have to put it into my trade journal. It was like I was looking over my own shoulder.

The judge and jury for my trades became my journal. I needed to make sure I had a strong case to defend my trade before I pulled the trigger.

- What is my trade plan?
- Is it conservative?

- What put me in?
- What took my out?
- What was the risk/reward ratio?
- Was this trade repeatable?

If I didn't have great answers to these questions, I didn't trade. I would be too embarrassed to enter a bad trade into my trade journal when I thought it had the potential to be bad. Because I entered all my trades into a journal, good or bad, I decided to not take the iffy trades.

After a while, I became quite surprised. I often seemed to sense I was going to make a mistake and by skipping the trade so I wouldn't have to enter it into my journal, I avoided a lot of bad trades! Perhaps half the time I thought I was going to make iffy trades and skipped them, they indeed turned out to be losers.

If you have ever made a stupid trade and knew it the second you pulled the trigger, you know exactly what I am talking about. Every trader I have ever spoken to has admitted to this. We all do it, hopefully only occasionally. I am happy to say that a trade journal is a device that prevents the vast majority of these stupid losing trades. Yes, you may talk yourself out of a few winning trades, but if your first priority is capital preservation, that is acceptable.

Missing some good trades because you lack confidence in the trade is acceptable because you'll miss a lot more bad trades. This will help you. You'll get better over time and will:

- Take control of your trading by planning your trades in advance and not chasing price.
- Begin to trade the same type of trade setups over and over again, developing some consistency to how you trade. You'll start with the ones that are easiest for you to spot and then with experience, begin to add to your trading repertoire.
- As you gain experience, you'll gain confidence in your trade planning abilities. This occurs because you only trade setups that you can plan ahead. Over time, pulling the trigger will get easier and easier as you prove to yourself that you have the skills to succeed in the world of forex.

The key to using a trade journal is to learn about how you trade, not what you traded. It's a way to critically observe your trading from a distance. See Figure 16.2.

Trade journals take a lot of effort. Most people will not keep a journal simply because it takes too much time. It's too much work to document each and every trade. They do not have the discipline to invest the time. They just want the quick and easy money of forex (ha, ha, ha). Guess

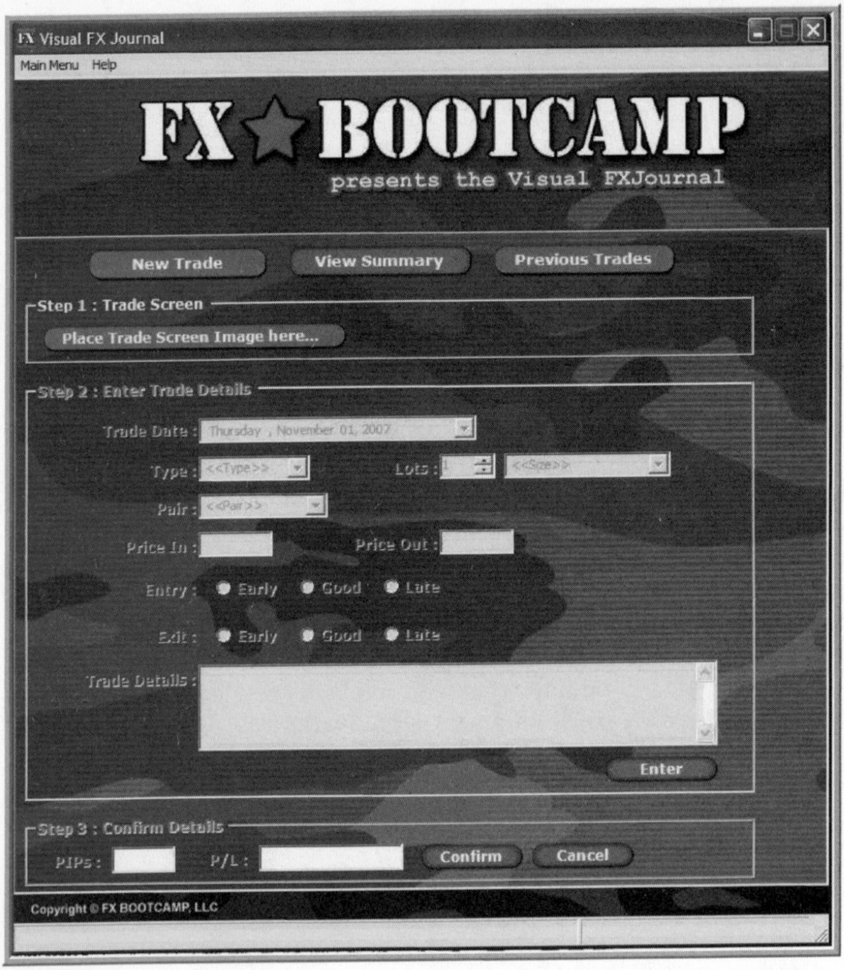

FIGURE 16.2 FX Journal
Source: FX Bootcamp, LLC (www.fxbootcamp.com)

who's going to be on the losing side of your winning trades? I promise you that keeping and using a trade journal properly will help you become a success.

There Is No Spoon

There is no oracle in forex. No one knows the future. Forex is fluid. Price always takes the path of least resistance. It goes up, down, or sideways based on the sum of an untold number of variables and a mix of objectives.

Opportunity for some traders to short is another trader's opportunity to go long. The only way to survive is to know how your trade plan fits into the whole scheme of things.

To do this, you need to know yourself and your trading abilities. The best way I found to analyze myself was to review my trades on a weekly basis.

Proof in the Pondering

Every Sunday evening, I printed out all the images from my trade journal so I could review them. This was usually about 20 pages, so it took a significant amount of my time. It was an investment.

This weekly exercise had two purposes:

1. It immediately tripled my trading experience. Now instead of living my trade once when I pulled the trigger, then living it again when I entered it into my trade journal, I was living the trade a third time when I reviewed it at the end of the week.

2. After reviewing the trades, I would identify my strengths and weaknesses as a trader. What was I doing right? What was I doing wrong? I would then write down one or two of the strengths and weaknesses I identified in my trading. These were my goals for the upcoming trading week.

I would continue to capture profits from fully realizing my strengths. More importantly however, I would make a conscious effort to improve my weaknesses.

If I was getting out of my trades too quickly last week, then this week I would work toward improving my exits and practice letting my profits run to more aggressive targets. It would be a clear goal and a focused objective in the coming week. Sometimes I even wrote the goals down on paper and taped them to my desk so I could always see them as I traded.

3X THE 4X

It was amazing how much this helped early in my career. Every time I made a trade I was actually learning from three trades. The upside was that I was getting 3 years of trading experience every 12 months. The downside was that it created a lot of work.

Trade → Review → Enter → Review → Print → Review

I began to trade less. Not only did I make fewer losing trades because I was only trading setups that had my utmost confidence based on trade planning, but when I did trade, it was a lot of work.

So I focused on trade planning, improving my confidence, refining my skills, and making more money—all by trading less. I honestly believe that all this work and effort did, in fact, develop positive trading habits. It was not a quick and easy process, but I did learn. What is important here is to note that it was all psychological. But the change it had on me was profound.

My fear shifted from losing money to having to enter a stupid trade in my trade journal. My greed to make money had turned into a game of discipline to do the right thing. The fundamental analysis was the same. The technical analysis was the same. However, everything changed when I committed 100 percent to forex—when I committed to strive for excellence as a trader.

SUMMARY

There may not be a perfect trader. No one was born to trade forex. However, it is the idea of striving for greatness that made a difference for me.

My simple goal was to pretend to be the trader I wanted to become for so long that perhaps one day I would forget I was pretending. I am not there yet, and perhaps I will never be. But I am certain that I am a better trader than I was, and I've enjoyed the journey tremendously.

It begs the questions:

- Do you know your strengths and weaknesses?
- Are you working on specific goals this week to improve as a trader?

CHAPTER 17

Target Practice

H ow do you review your trades? Relive your trades.
At the end of each trading week, print out all your trade entries. Each trade will have its own page, including all the financial details, your trading notes, and an image of your charts. When you are done with your printouts, put them into a book; you never know, you may need them one day during a tax audit.

Now, take a second blank piece of paper, a book, or anything that will cover the image of your chart. You should not be able to see through to your chart image. The idea is for you to run through your trade—again for the first time. Your mind will not know the difference. See Figure 17.1.

Move the cover paper from left to right, displaying one candle at a time. What are the moving averages doing? What is the speed and momentum? Are the oscillators agreeing or not? Redo the trade and critique how you handled the trade in reality.

You are trying to identify your trading strengths and weaknesses. Most importantly, after reviewing all your trades from the previous week, you know exactly what to improve upon this coming week.

Write down the things you will strive to improve upon in the coming five trading days. Tape them near your computer screen so you can see the goals as you trade. Don't print them, write them. You will internalize the goals mentally, visually, and even tactilely. The more forms of input the better. For example:

"I will wait for price to pull back, or I will let the trade go."

"I will always take profit at S2 and R2."

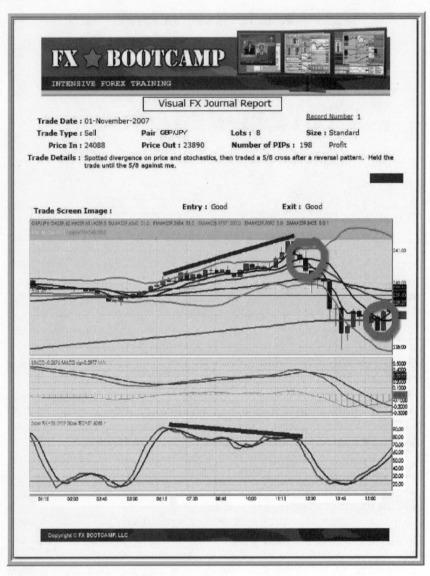

FIGURE 17.1 Sample Journal Entry
Source: FX Bootcamp, LLC (www.fxbootcamp.com)

"I will take the loss when the charts tell me to get out. I take pride in exiting for small losses."

"I will look for reasons to sell at resistance and to buy at support or create a breakout trade plan."

"I will not force the market to move."

"I will never revenge trade."

"Uptrends: M2 to M4, downtrends: M3 to M1, range: R1 to S1."

"38.2 percent to 161.8 percent, 61.8 percent to 138.2 percent, 78.6 percent to 121.4 percent."

"I will move my stop loss to protect minimal acceptable performance and then stay in the trade until momentum crosses against me."

"I will not risk more than my business plan allows me to."

Let's do some target practicing now by reviewing Figures 17.2 through 17.13. On one side of the page, you will see charts with only half the candles visible. On the next page, you will see the results. I will show various pairs and time frames. It is a good idea to take this information into account.

SUMMARY

Remember, this is just like the exercise you should be doing each week. It is an easy and safe way to refine your trading skills. Most, if not the vast majority of traders, are not willing to do this much work to achieve success. Are you? Is this too hard to do? Are you willing to invest an hour a week to do this? I was amazed how much it helped me.

It works because your mind doesn't know the difference and therefore you can count it as real trading experience. By doing this exercise, you are building positive trading habits and skills.

Mental outlook is also important to your success. Have you thought about your trading six months from now? How about a year from now? Will you be successful? How do you know? You can't know unless you measure.

For me, moving from a "must make money today" to a long-term plan was paramount. It helped me to see my trading as a business, manage my risk, and understand how every single day is just a small part of my future. What happens on any given day is not that important in the long run. Developing a three-year plan elevated me from a novice day trader into a professional career.

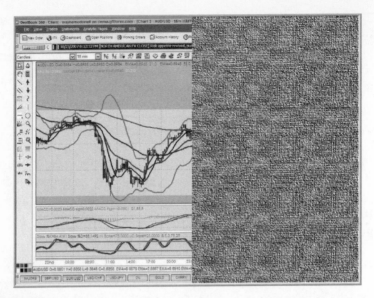

FIGURE 17.2 Before 1
Source: FX Bootcamp, LLC (www.fxbootcamp.com)
DealBook® 360 screen capture printed by permission. © 2008 by Global Forex Trading, Ada MI USA

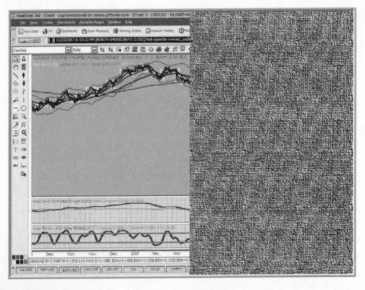

FIGURE 17.3 Before 2
Source: FX Bootcamp, LLC (www.fxbootcamp.com)
DealBook® 360 screen capture printed by permission. © 2008 by Global Forex Trading, Ada MI USA

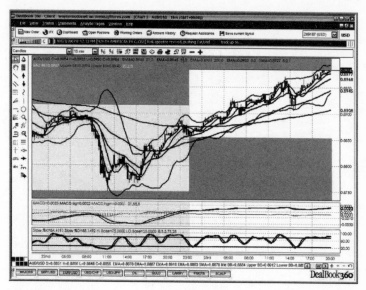

FIGURE 17.4 After 1

Source: FX Bootcamp, LLC (www.fxbootcamp.com)
DealBook® 360 screen capture printed by permission. © 2008 by Global Forex Trading, Ada MI USA

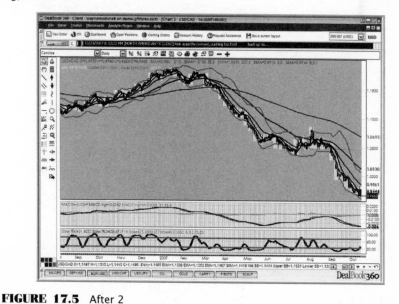

FIGURE 17.5 After 2

Source: FX Bootcamp, LLC (www.fxbootcamp.com)
DealBook® 360 screen capture printed by permission. © 2008 by Global Forex Trading, Ada MI USA

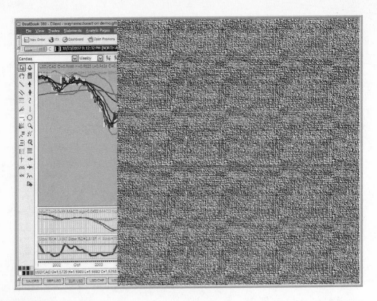

FIGURE 17.6 Before 3
Source: FX Bootcamp, LLC (www.fxbootcamp.com)
DealBook® 360 screen capture printed by permission. © 2008 by Global Forex Trading, Ada MI USA

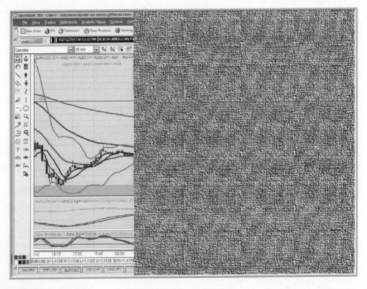

FIGURE 17.7 Before 4
Source: FX Bootcamp, LLC (www.fxbootcamp.com)
DealBook® 360 screen capture printed by permission. © 2008 by Global Forex Trading, Ada MI USA

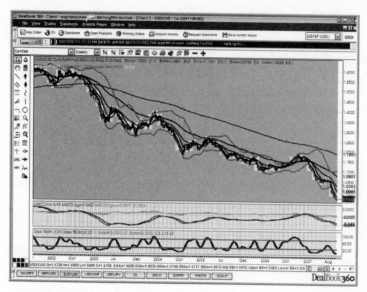

FIGURE 17.8 After 3
Source: FX Bootcamp, LLC (www.fxbootcamp.com)
DealBook® 360 screen capture printed by permission. © 2008 by Global Forex Trading, Ada MI USA

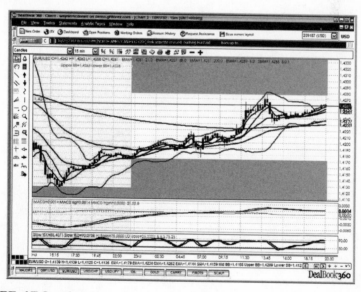

FIGURE 17.9 After 4
Source: FX Bootcamp, LLC (www.fxbootcamp.com)
DealBook® 360 screen capture printed by permission. © 2008 by Global Forex Trading, Ada MI USA

FIGURE 17.10 Before 5
Source: FX Bootcamp, LLC (www.fxbootcamp.com)
DealBook® 360 screen capture printed by permission. © 2008 by Global Forex Trading, Ada MI USA

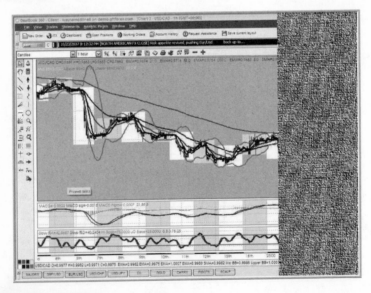

FIGURE 17.11 Before 6
Source: FX Bootcamp, LLC (www.fxbootcamp.com)
DealBook® 360 screen capture printed by permission. © 2008 by Global Forex Trading, Ada MI USA

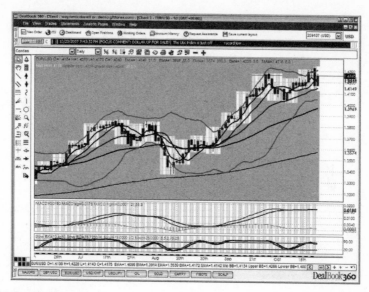

FIGURE 17.12 After 5

Source: FX Bootcamp, LLC (www.fxbootcamp.com)
DealBook® 360 screen capture printed by permission. © 2008 by Global Forex Trading, Ada MI USA

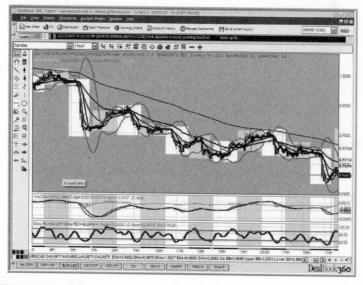

FIGURE 17.13 After 6

Source: FX Bootcamp, LLC (www.fxbootcamp.com)
DealBook® 360 screen capture printed by permission. © 2008 by Global Forex Trading, Ada MI USA

CHAPTER 18

Three-Year Plan

I f you have any doubts about the power of minimal acceptable performance (MAP), planning your trading will be the proof you need to ac-
knowledge the powerful results that conservative and repeatable trading can provide.

During a press conference, Albert Einstein was asked by a reporter,
"What is the most powerful force in the universe?" Einstein responded,
"Compound interest!"

The general theory of minimal acceptable performance (MAP) takes
a similar approach to Einstein's point in response to the reporter's question. Small gains over a long period of time can really grow into something
impressive.

FX BUSINESS PLANNER

Let's take a look at the FX Business Planner and how it illustrates this
concept. However, please don't lose sight of what it is trying to say. The
application may tell you that you could theoretically make a trillion dollars
per year. Well, isn't that crazy? Yes it is. What it is really telling you is that
you are taking far too much risk per trade and you should lower it. When
using the FX Business Planner, and whenever trading forex for that matter,
don't focus on the money; focus on the risk.

The FX Business Planner has two goals:

1. Provide evidence that you can be a conservative trader and still be financially successful. You don't need to be aggressive.
2. You can afford to lower your risk.

The ideal starting point for all novice traders who are planning their future trading businesses is to target the income level they need to achieve in their trading to be able to afford to quit their day jobs. This is not a focus on financial freedom, but on freedom to trade forex as a full-time trader.

What is your current income or an income you need to live comfortably? Focus on achieving this level and maintaining this level for the next three years. This will help you focus on developing your trading skills (skill denotes a long-term ability) and grow your trading account.

The FX Business Planner takes a few variables into account and then illustrates MAP everyday over the course of the next three years: day by day, week by week, year by year. It will show you:

- Your daily income.
- The number of mini-lots to trade.
- Your annual income.
- The size of your trading account.

The variables include:

- The size of your opening trade account.
- The amount of risk you assume.
- How much profit you pay yourself.

The FX Business Planner (as shown in Figure 18.1) assumes that you achieve MAP on a daily basis. Remember, its primary goal is to prove that a daily minimal acceptable performance, even though relatively small, really mounts up. I hope this puts your daily focus on achieving MAP.

Minimal acceptable performance is only 15 pips. However, it is not a goal. You are not trying to get 15 pips. You are trying to put yourself into trading situations where, if things don't work out as well as you planned, you still walk away with MAP.

In a typical spot trade on a 15-minute chart, a reasonable trade setup should likely yield 30 to 45 pips. Therefore, even if your entry or exit isn't perfect, you should still easily walk away with MAP or better.

Another way of looking at MAP is as a daily average. Do you think it is a reasonable goal to average 15 pips per day or better? The GBP/USD

FIGURE 18.1 FX Business Planner
Source: FX Bootcamp, LLC (www.fxbootcamp.com)

moves 130 pips a day, and the GBP/JPY moves 230 pips a day. Is 15 pips realistic and achievable on a daily basis? I think so.

Therefore, if MAP is your focus, then you can afford to skip trade setups you are not confident in. You can wait. Create another plan. It's better to miss a trade than to lose money. There *will* be another trade. The concept of MAP will liberate your trading and actually remove stress.

In fact, you can even skip entire trading days. If the market is quiet and you're already up 125 pips for the week, don't force a trade. Take the day off. Now, isn't that liberating!

The way to make this work is getting more than MAP. Remember, MAP is your minimum goal. For your average to work, your trading average should cover all of your losing trades and days you don't trade at all.

This is exactly why you need to turn aggressive after you have locked in MAP. With your stop loss protecting your 15-pip profit, you must grab every pip you can. You need big wins now and then to cover your not-so-stellar days. So the FX Business Planner assumes a profit of 15 pips per day. You cannot assume you will make 15 pips a day, but an average of 15 pips a day is very achievable.

After year three is done, you may want to raise it, but until then, focus on developing your skills. Remember, it's the mind-set and the work you do now that will make you successful later. Cut corners here and you will pay later.

Stay humble regarding your charts and your trading. Don't get too confident. Forex has a way of crushing your confidence. Therefore, just do the work, and strive for greatness in the long-term as a conservative trader looking for repeatable trades.

With the simple focus of reaching your comfortable income level, let's say $125,000 per year, all you are trying to achieve is that income for the next three years. Each year you will lower your risk just enough to maintain that income. As time goes by, you will live a comfortable life while lowering your risk more and more.

After the first three years of your trading business has passed (most traders don't even get through their first year), you will find that your risk is actually quite low and your trading account quite large—in fact, it'll be growing quickly now.

In year four and five you won't need to lower your risk any more, but your income will be growing like the most powerful force in the universe: compound interest. It's called exponential growth. You will deserve this success, as 95 percent of traders are just not willing to work that hard for that long. They will quit and try the next get-rich-quick scheme.

To illustrate the values of conservative trading, please note that there is a strange paradox in planning your trading business three years in advance. The less you pay yourself, for example 33 percent vs. 40 percent of your trading profits, the more money you actually make. This is because the size of your trading account grows and the number of lots you can afford increases down the road. Isn't that cool?

RISK MANAGEMENT

Another side to managing the psychological aspects of trading takes the form of risk control. I have found that new traders, including myself when I first ventured into forex, trade too often and with too many lots. With too much money at stake, perhaps from greed, fear begins to creep into your trading.

Each individual trade should have almost no bearing on your long-term success. If you are sweating bullets or "need this to win," you will certainly lose in the long run. Eventually, your luck will run dry along with your trading account.

Trigger Happy

Trade planning and keeping a trade journal will likely have a calming effect on your trading. If done properly, it means you will miss some trades because you didn't plan for them or you'll skip others if they just don't seem certain enough to be worth facing the judge and jury of your journal.

This will naturally bring consistency to your trading. You are consistently avoiding the trades you are not too sure about and trading the ones you are. You are repeating, refining, and building your trade skills. Trade by trade, session by session, day by day, week by week, month by month, and year by year, you are becoming a conservative and repeatable trader.

The next step will be to expand your constancy beyond your trading and add it to each of your trades by consistently managing risk. As each of your individual trades becomes more consistent in terms of risk, your emotions will become less and less of an issue, because your trades will become more and more the same.

Over the years, I've seen novice traders make a couple of common mistakes when managing their risk:

1. They always trade the same number of lots.
2. They always trade with the same stop loss.

It is consistent, but they are essentially not managing their risk at all. Both are variables that should be adjusted according to the trade setup in your trade plan.

I adjust the number of lots traded based upon how far my stop loss is placed from my entry. The goal is to make every trade the same amount of risk. This is the consistency I seek. Not every trade setup is the same, but ideally the risk you take should be.

How to Manage Risk

1. Define your entry price.
2. Define your stop price.
3. Define your risk tolerance.
4. Calculate your trade budget.

This should be done for each of your trades. The trade budget is the number of lots you can afford to place on this particular trade to make it consistent with all your other trades in terms of risk.

The end result is that psychologically, trade risk becomes a constant, and you are never nervous about any particular trade because you have too much money riding on the outcome. Every trade, in terms of risk, becomes the same, regardless of the potential risk of loss.

The number of pips will be different on each trade, but the value of the potential loss (risk) will be the same. Because you adjust the number of lots you trade based on your stop loss placement, a 33-pip loss that equals a $1,000 loss would be the same as a 50-pip loss that equals $1,000. The trade with a 50-pip stop loss simply had fewer lots invested in the trade.

The only variable you need to know in advance is the percent of risk you are willing to risk. To truly understand what this means, you need to take a long-term view of your trading. This is why we use the FX Business Planner. Hopefully your long-term plan will carry more weight than your short-term desire to make some fast money. See Figure 18.2.

Trade Your Budget

This is key. You will find this more difficult to do when you are starting to become consistent with your trading. Once you begin to trade well, you will be tempted to increase your lots.

This is exactly opposite what I am advising you to do. I'm advising you to avoid the temptation to make money. Focus on developing your skills for the first three years. As you do so, I want you to ratchet down your risk, not spike it up. You may say, "Wayne, I'm making 50 pips a day. Why shouldn't I load the boat?"

It's completely a mind game. My focus is on the long term. I'm not trying to hit home runs, find the mother lode, and strike it rich quick. I am trying to make small, conservative, and repeatable trades over and over and over and over and over and over and over and over and over again.

I have seen members of FX Bootcamp lose sight of this modest goal and they have paid the price. They increase the lot sizes and start to make big money. Greed creeps in. The trader cuts corners, getting in a little early to catch the entire move. Why not? He's on a roll! Then one day he really bets the farm and loads the boat; he ends up buying a first-class ticket on the *Titanic*. He is sunk.

Humble yourself to your charts. Humble yourself to your business plan. Humble yourself to MAP.

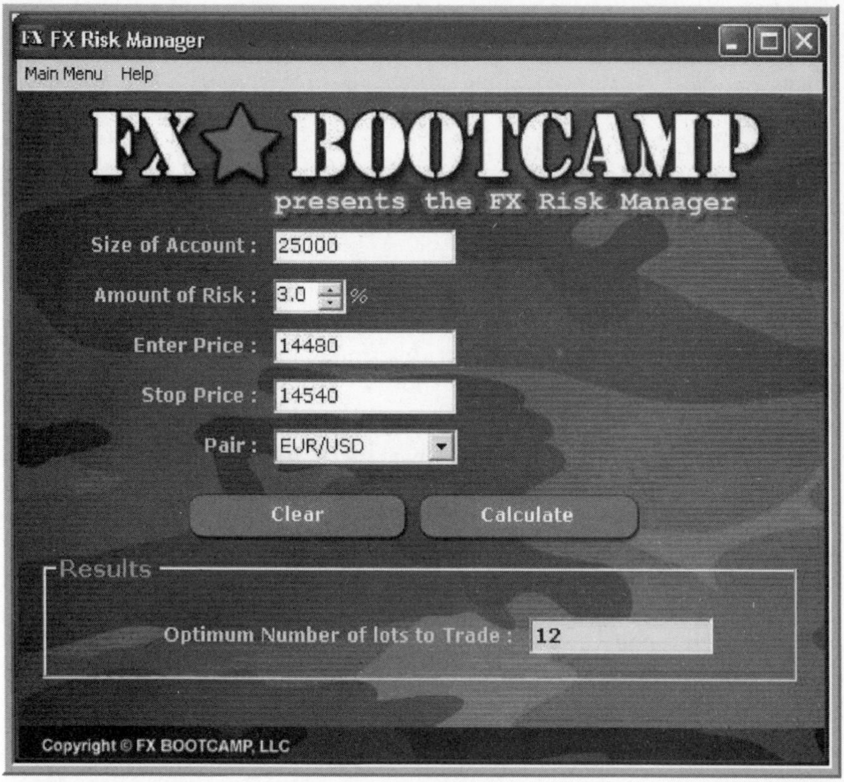

FIGURE 18.2 FX Risk Manager
Source: FX Bootcamp, LLC (www.fxbootcamp.com)

Stay small as long as possible. If you really are a good trader, forex will always be here for you. What's the rush? Why take the risk when you are still learning the ropes? If you were to make big, silly, stupid mistakes (and we all have), they are more likely to happen early in your career. Focus on developing your skills now so you don't crash and burn later.

I have always found it a challenge. I just wish I knew this focus was the name of the game back when I first started trading forex. It took a lot of blood, sweat, and tears to figure it out. It's not the trading but the discipline to stay in control of your trading that makes you a success.

Imagine, if you are having trouble with the psychological aspects of trading your $5,000 account, how do you expect to succeed long term to trade your $5,000,000 account? Practice now. It will not get easier. Do the work now. Resist the temptation to make money now. Become a skilled and disciplined trader, and the money will take care of itself.

Avoid the Revenge Trade

"An eye for an eye," Gandhi remarked, "will make the whole world go
blind."

The worst of the worst thing you can possibly do in forex is to trade
out of anger. And the worst of the worst thing that can happen is that you
make money doing it.

A revenge trade is a trade that is made right after a big loss that makes
you angry, frustrated, or otherwise upset. They often occur immediately
after the loss. They are not set up with a trade plan but created purely out
of emotion.

If you feel like trading out of revenge, you have done something terribly wrong. How could your recent loss be so great that you are actually
angry about it? You can't possibly be upset about a small trade, right? Then
the mistake was that you did not follow your plan. Therefore, trading to
avenge the loss is not appropriate. The market did not make the mistake.
You did.

For you to be so upset as to make a trade based on emotion, you either
had too much money invested in the trade, or you did not exit when you
should have and the loss was too big. In either case, you should punish
yourself by redoing some training.

Bad Medicine

A typical bonehead revenge trade happens when you take a big loss and
follow it up, often within seconds, with another stupid trade. Here is how I
personally make this revenge trade.

It usually occurs when I enter my first trade late. I got in with
fuzzy logic, but the trade seems certain to want to continue anyway.
But it doesn't. The late entry quickly puts me in a losing situation, let's
say down 30 pips. Crap! So I exit the trade and immediately invest the
other way. No plan other than that I was wrong in the first plan. The
fuzzy logic is that if price is not going to fall, it's going to rise, right?
Wrong again.

What the %$#%? When this happens, please recognize that you broke
many common rules of conservative trading. The perfect trader certainly
would not have traded that way. So take a break, clear your mind, and
return to the charts later. Rake some leaves. Walk your dog. Call an old
friend you haven't talked to in a while. Soak up some good karma and come
back when you are ready to strive for excellence.

Recurring Nightmare

However, the worst-case scenario is when a revenge trade turns profitable. There can be no worse curse placed on you, and you cursed yourself, because it will cost you a lot more money in the long run.

A revenge trade that you lose money on is a learning experience you don't soon forget. Not only did you do something stupid in the first place to make you so upset as to trade in revenge, but you followed it up immediately with another trade even more stupid than the first. At some point, I hope you throw in the towel.

I am sure we have all been there before. It's painful. Like a slap—no punch—in the face. But it is a wake-up call. You say to yourself, "Two bad trades in row? What am I going to do about this?"

A call to arms has been made and a new strategy with new tactics is made. "Back to conservative trading!" you pledge.

However, what happens if you revenge trade *and* make money doing it? You are doomed to repeat the costly mistake over and over again. Here's how the nightmare unfolds:

1. You place a trade and you are up 20 pips. You say to yourself that when you are up to 25 pips profit, you will move your stop to breakeven and remove risk.
2. Price bounces around 15 and 22 pips profit for a long time.
3. Suddenly, price moves against you and you are −10 pips in the hole. But just as you reach for your mouse, price pops again and you are only down −2 pips. You say to yourself, "Why get out now, I am still in this trade and it looks like it should come back."
4. Price sits here for a while. A moving average is getting closer and closer. Soon, it will push your trade back into profit.
5. The moving average fails. Price moves and you are quickly −22 pips in the hole. "Oh no! How did that happen? I was up 20 and now I am down 22. Son of a . . ."
6. Now −30, −38. "Crap."
7. It's at the next moving average that's just got to hold. I can't get out now, it's back at resistance. I'll let it retrace and try to get out with just a −20-pip loss.
8. Finally! Red, beautiful red candles!
9. −20 pips. Why get out now, it's coming back and looking great. "This was sort of like another trade plan," you say to yourself reassuringly.

"I should be able to ride this back to breakeven. In fact, this trade is starting to look great again."

10. Back to breakeven and now +5. "I'm the *man*! I called it! See, it pays to have the guts to stay with your trade!"

11. Oh no, −3! I don't want to go through this again. How could I be so stupid?

12. +1. Out. "Wow, what a ride."

Sound familiar? This kind of trading will wear you out. You will *not* be able to do this in the long run.

The story gets worse. It's much easier to build bad habits than good ones. A successful revenge trade always turns into a bad soap opera. The next time a trader finds himself in this kind of situation, he has reinforced his fallacious strategy with poor trading experience. However, the trader isn't so lucky. Instead of trading out of the situation, he rides it back even farther to a much worse trade and with a big loss.

But that was just bad luck. So he does it again on another trade and loses again. Then again. Then again. Now he throws in the towel. Not in the first round when he was relatively unhurt, but in the 10th round when the pain is much worse.

Imagine how a boxer would feel if he got beat up for 10 rounds and loses at the close of the match to a decision. Hey, it was a close match. The boxer showed a lot of heart. Perhaps won some respect. But at the end of the day, he lost, and the bruises always hurt more when you don't win.

SUMMARY

Your trading can be a career. You can trade your own money and try to build a vast amount of wealth. You can trade as a retirement income as you enjoy your golden years. You can trade other people's money (OPM). You could even trade forex in a corporation or in a bank.

In any case, in my opinion, if you do not develop a long-term plan for your forex career then you plan to fail as a forex trader. In that case, perhaps you should go after that marketing position you saw advertised online. Maybe they'll give you a nice cubicle to work in. If you keep your head down and make yourself look busy, you'll get through the day, week, and month. You'll earn your paycheck every couple of weeks no matter what the market does. Maybe your boss will even buy you a lunch every so often. Life will be easy as you live a quiet life of desperation. Enjoy the commute!

If you don't like the sound of that, then let me remind you about what Sun Tzu said in the *Art of War*:

> "Planning is a great matter to a general [trader];
> it is the ground of death and of life;
> it is the way of survival and of destruction,
> and must be examined . . ."

Will you plan to succeed or fail to plan? What about the 95 percent of novice traders who lose money; what do they do? I'd venture to guess that the vast majority of them not only do not plan their trades in advance, but they also don't have a long-term plan for their trading career, either.

I suppose that is okay by me. They add liquidity to my trades. Remember, forex is a zero-sum game. If I am going to extract money from the forex market, then somebody will have to take the losing end of my profitable trade. It could be a billionaire hedge fund manager who doesn't care about my little trades, or it could be the novice trader who didn't buy this book. In any case, somebody has to lose. I just hope it's not you.

PART FIVE SUMMARY

To recap, following are the key takeaways for Part Five:

- Forex is not just technicals or fundamentals.
- Trading success comes from understanding human behavior—including your own.
- Our acceptance of risk in exchange for big rewards is our greatest weakness.
- Hedge fund managers and bankers trade differently from retail trader, and they control the market.
- Do not trade against them. Trade with them.
- Logic can fail. Just follow the leaders or get out of their way.
- This discipline to do this will take a 100 percent commitment from you. Forex is not easy.
- It will take a lot of work, energy, and time, as no one was born to trade.
- Trade journals help you relive your trades and gain additional experience.
- Journals help you to identify your strengths and weaknesses.
- Journals will make you trade less.
- Journals will make you trade consistently.

- Treat your trading like a business.
- Create a three-year trading business plan.
- Over time, reduce your risk and grow your account.
- Manage risk by budgeting your money.
- Let bad trades go. Do not avenge them.
- Never trade alone.

CHAPTER 19

Closing Notes

T his book has given you a lot of advice. I hope you learned a little about the who, what, when, and why of forex. I hope this book helps your trading somehow. I really do.

For some people, however, there may still be a missing piece. I would have been one of those people. Let me tell you a little story about myself.

THE GENESIS OF FX BOOTCAMP

I traded forex on demo accounts for over two years, and at first I was pretty bad at it. Looking back, I'm astonished at how little I knew.

I traded and I traded. I bought a few e-books. I bought a few DVDs. Not much helped. Some were more confusing than helpful. I played with every technical indicator. I even messed around with their settings. Some things worked some of the time.

My typical day started with me waking up very early in the morning and trading on my laptop. I would do this for a few hours. Then in 15 minutes flat I would shower, eat breakfast, and jump in the car to go to work.

I would watch the market action on my cell phone while sitting in rush hour traffic near the city. I would eventually get to the parking lot and either walk the rest of the way to the office or wait for the shuttle. Either way, my eyes were glued to the cell phone and the forex prices.

Eventually I would get to work. I had a micro laptop. It had a 10-inch screen and weighed less than a pound. It would sit on the corner of my desk with my forex charts open. I would watch it all day. Even in meetings, I had one eye on the conversation and one eye on the charts. Luckily I did not go cross-eyed!

This went on for a long time. Slowly, I got to be a better trader. I was showing a lot of improvement. Then improvement led to hope. "Perhaps I can do this after all!"

It would have been a lot easier and a lot less painful if someone had just showed me how to trade in the first place. Why did I have to reinvent the wheel? I wished I could have stood on the shoulders of a giant.

Now that I was becoming a fairly good trader, my goal was to make much more money on my demo account than in my real-world job. If I could trade forex on a consistent basis, I would quit my job and trade forex full time.

This was not an easy decision, however, as I loved my job. I really did. As far as I was concerned, my job was perfect for me. But I got to a point where forex was such a distraction that I had to make a decision: Love it or leave it.

So I really started to take my trading seriously. This was the real deal now. I had to trade my demo account like it was real money. It was a nervous time. There was even talk of the EUR reaching parity with the USD. Can you imagine!

After several months of great success, I quit my job and went into forex trading full time. What a glorious time. It was liberating and frightening. It was like a roller-coaster ride; simply thrilling.

But I ran into some challenges that I did not expect. I did not see them coming. I started making silly mistakes. I had started out just fine, but now I was having trouble. What was different? The difference between trading at the office downtown and trading in my home office was the isolation. I was lonely. I was trading from 10:00 P.M. to 10:00 A.M. California time.

My sleep patterns were thrown off. It was dark all the time. I had to be quiet so I did not wake my wife up. I didn't have anyone to high-five when I made a great trade. I didn't have anyone to give me a kick when I did something wrong.

Forex began to lack life and energy. My trading suffered. I was used to working at the firm with hundreds of employees. Now I was all by myself. I needed to be around other traders. I needed their energy and I wanted to give them mine. My quest was to build synergy and create a team of like-minded forex traders.

But how would I do that?

My solution was to share everything I head learned: the good, the bad, and the ugly. I realized that because I tended to be an overachiever, I just wouldn't give up—even when I probably should have. By working harder than 95 percent of new traders, I found a way to survive.

I wasn't better than anyone else; I just didn't give up. I was lucky to have a job that I liked before forex. I was not in a hurry to quit. Others are not so fortunate. They need forex to work quickly. It never does. They push hard for quick success and end up blowing through their account and give up. I wanted to see if I could prevent that.

In war movies, you often see new, clean-cut recruits who arrive in the war zone for the first time. They are nervous and wide eyed. They are totally overwhelmed and out of place. Then they meet their noncommissioned officer. He is the real deal: He is dirty, battle scarred, and full of advice:

"Never salute me. Snipers would love to grease an officer. Keep your canteen full or they will hear you coming from a mile away. Don't wear bug spray or they will smell you coming. Keep your head down. Put tape on your dog tags and watch. Pack three pairs of socks." And on and on.

Your noncomm was the most qualified soldier to lead, not because he was better, but because he was the only one to not get killed. You followed him because you trusted him. He'd keep you alive. He never gave an order he would not carry out himself. If you stayed close to him and did what he said, you'd learn to stay alive, too.

That's what my idea was for FX Bootcamp. I would build a community centered around keeping traders alive throughout their first year, perhaps beyond. No magic formula or strategy to pitch. FX Bootcamp would just be about how to trade and not get yourself killed. I would be the officer who would lead from the trenches in the mud and the first to charge out of the foxhole.

I would just teach others how to trade. They would still make their own trading decisions, but I would teach them how to think for themselves. I figured that there were many traders who could grasp what I learned, but they simply gave up because they couldn't filter through all the bad information.

I know it took me a very long time to learn how to trade forex—well into the thousands of hours realm. But if someone would have just showed me how to trade, I could have learned much faster and would have made a lot fewer mistakes.

I didn't want someone to trade for me. I just needed a guide to show me how to trade for myself.

LEAD BY EXAMPLE

I would be the battle-scarred soldier who kept people alive. I would share everything I learned by trading. I would show them how to stay alive. I would talk to them as they traded, provide encouragement or feedback, and drill home lessons over and over and over again.

It had to be live or it wouldn't work. FX Bootcamp could not be just the theory of how to trade forex. It had to be the practice of how to trade forex successfully everyday.

I would surround myself with a team of traders all around the world and we'd trade together. A "band of brothers" who would keep each other alive with the same focus:

1. Survive at all costs.
2. Achieve the mission.
3. Win the war.

It worked. FX Bootcamp members now come from more than 50 different countries. Bootcampers are men and women. There are 75–year-olds and 18-year-olds. Some have $500 trading accounts; others have accounts worth millions. Everyone is represented on our team.

We have built a great support system and an amazing community. In fact, there are happy FX Bootcampers who have been members for years and remain members just for the community aspect. They've made friends and have a good time.

So I know my vision has beccome a great success. I started FX Bootcamp because I did not want to trade alone. Now I see members who don't want to leave, because they don't want to trade alone, either. In that respect, with FX Bootcamp, we all win.

For FX Bootcampers who first learned how to survive, then became successful traders, and now stay active in our community, in my humble opinion, the war is over for them. For as forex traders, they've found peace.

ADDITIONAL SUPPORT

Thank you for investing your time and money into this book. I hope it has been helpful and will positively impact your currency trading.

Feel free to access the companion web site for this book (at www.fxbootcamp.com/book).

The companion site has charts and videos that go along with the examples in this book. I will also host free "How To" webinars from time to time for readers who sign up. This will provide an opportunity for me to answer any questions you may have. I'm sure you have a few. Thanks again.

I hope to see you online soon. Remember, you either plan to win or fail to plan.

Happy pipp'n!

Wayne McDonell
Chief Currency Coach
FX Bootcamp, LLC
www.fxbootcamp.com

BOOK BUYBACK PROGRAM

If you are like me and don't want to trade forex alone, become a new member of FX Bootcamp. You can trade with us every day. If you do sign up, I will buy your book back from you. You can keep your copy of the book. I'll just reimburse you for your purchase.

For more details, log on to: www.fxbootcamp.com/book

Index